# 100 THINGS
# RED SOX FANS
## SHOULD KNOW & DO
## BEFORE THEY DIE

# 100 THINGS RED SOX FANS SHOULD KNOW & DO BEFORE THEY DIE

Nick Cafardo

TRIUMPH
BOOKS

Triumph Books and colophon are registered trademarks of Random House, Inc.

Library of Congress Cataloging-in-Publication Data

Cafardo, Nick.
    100 things Red Sox fans should know and do before they die / Nick Cafardo.
        p. cm.
    ISBN-13: 978-1-60078-053-0
    ISBN-10: 1-60078-053-9
    1. Boston Red Sox (Baseball team)—Anecdotes. 2. Boston Red Sox (Baseball team)—Miscellanea. I. Title. II. Title: One hundred things Red Sox fans should know and do before they die.
    GV875.B62C34 2008
    796.357'640974461—dc22
                                                                        2008006191

This book is available in quantity at special discounts for your group or organization. For further information, contact:
    **Triumph Books**
    542 South Dearborn Street
    Suite 750
    Chicago, Illinois 60605
    (312) 939-3330
    Fax (312) 663-3557

Printed in U.S.A.
ISBN: 978-1-60078-053-0
Design by Patricia Frey
All photos courtesy of Getty Images unless otherwise indicated.

*To Leeanne, Ben, and Emilee. Their love and support enabled me to pursue this lifelong Red Sox thing.*

*To my Dad, Nicola. My brother, Fred, and I lost him at the beginning of 2008, but we will never forget the pleasure and happiness he experienced watching every single Red Sox game and the contentment he felt when his beloved team won two championships before he died.*

# Contents

# Foreword

Officially I spent 143 days with the Red Sox in 2004, from July 31 to December 20. Doesn't seem like a long time, but in that short period I came away with the greatest memories of my major league career.

The impact of stealing second base against Mariano Rivera in the ninth inning of Game 4 against the Yankees didn't sink in until we came back from that 0–3 deficit and beat the Yankees in the 2004 ALCS and then went on to sweep the St. Louis Cardinals for the World Series title. Those victories broke an 86-year curse. I now understand the magnitude of what happened, and I am constantly reminded of the steal and its place in Red Sox history.

I am so proud to have been a part of it. Listen, I understand this was a huge team effort. I got myself into scoring position, but Bill Mueller drove me in to tie the game and gave us a chance. We took it from there. We had to win Game 4 in the bottom of the twelfth on a two-run walk-off home run by David Ortiz off Tom Gordon in an incredible moment—it was an incredible clutch hit by Big Papi. I'll never forget the electricity in Fenway Park that night. Who could ever forget that?

Our attitude was: take it one by one. I still remember Kevin Millar in the clubhouse just going up to everybody and saying, "It's one game. One game." We never thought of it as being down three games. We took every game and tried to win that night.

We had the right combination of players—a great chemistry on that team to pull it off. It was a group of professionals who never succumbed to pressure. We had players who didn't know what pressure was. We had guys like Pedro Martinez, Curt Schilling, Derek Lowe, Keith Foulke, and Mike Timlin on our pitching staff. We had Johnny Damon and Millar, Jason Varitek, Manny Ramirez, David Ortiz, Billy Mueller, Todd Walker, Orlando Cabrera, Trot Nixon. On and

*Dave Roberts hoists the trophy in celebration after the Red Sox defeated the St. Louis Cardinals 3–0 in Game 4 of the World Series on October 27, 2004, at Busch Stadium in St. Louis.*

on. We had players with grit and determination. It was the greatest story of perseverance I'd ever been a part of. It was the greatest story of never say never. It was the greatest story of a team with their backs against the wall and everyone thought there was no hope except for the 25 guys in the clubhouse who each and every day would pat each other on the back and just remind one another that we can do this.

I come back to Boston every year for signings, and I'm constantly reminded of how special that steal was and what it meant for thousands of Red Sox fans in Red Sox Nation. I've played in a lot of places—big-time baseball cities. I played in Cleveland when they were perennial playoff contenders. I've played in Los Angeles with the Dodgers. I currently play in San Francisco, where baseball is very important. But nothing will ever compare to the intensity, the passion people have for baseball in Boston.

I felt it the moment I stepped foot in Fenway Park after I'd been traded from Los Angeles. I had been a starter for a first-place team, but I was coming to Boston to be a role player. That's usually not the greatest situation for a ballplayer. You don't want to go from starting to sitting on the bench, but I knew when I came over that it was the chance of a lifetime.

We had guys who all knew their roles. We had guys who made sacrifices for the greater good of the team. We had brought Doug Mientkievicz over from Minnesota. Dougie had been a starting player, too, and his role was going to be to serve as a defensive replacement for Kevin Millar at first base. Dougie was in the same boat I was, but we accepted it from day one. Then there was Gabe Kapler, who really served an important role both on the field and in the clubhouse.

Terry Francona explained what he expected from us in order for this to work. And we made it work. We created an excitement around Fenway and around the country with our style of play. We gained momentum that got us into the playoffs, and I got to witness firsthand how intense it was being a player for the Red Sox and how intense that Red Sox–Yankees rivalry is. Until you experience it firsthand, you don't really know.

I loved every minute of it. I played 45 regular-season games for Boston, but it's funny—I probably remember all of them because it was so unique. I only appeared in three games in all the playoffs in '04 and never set foot on the field for the World Series. Yet so much happened. So many memories. It's really hard to put it into words, but over time, with the continued attention I get everywhere I go, I realize that what happened that October 17 night at Fenway made an impact not only in Boston but all across America. It's really surreal. It was such a humbling experience to receive so much notoriety and attention for one play. When I look at the footage of it, I still get goose bumps.

I did so much studying of video leading up to it. I watched Mariano Rivera's delivery and really broke it down with our first-base coach, Lynn Jones. By the time I got out there on the base path, I was ready. I knew what I had to do, and based on the video I had studied, I knew when I had to do it. So many things have to go right in stealing a base, especially in that situation. You have to be safe. You just have to be.

Maury Wills once told me there will come a point in my career when everyone in the ballpark will know that I have to steal a base, and I will steal that base. When I got out there, I knew that was what Maury Wills had been talking about.

People often ask me if I would have enjoyed playing in Boston longer. Of course I would have. But at that point in my career I believed I was still an everyday player, and I wanted the chance to return to being an everyday player. I thank Theo Epstein for giving me the chance to do that again. He traded me to San Diego that winter. I grew up on the West Coast. My family is out here, and my kids go to school here. Anyway, I'm not sure anything I would have done in Boston after that stolen base would ever compare, and I'm perfectly content leaving that as my long-lasting memory.

I cheered for the Red Sox in '07 when they won it all again. Some people have said to me that maybe winning in '07 took away from what we accomplished in '04. But I don't think so. That was the first championship in 86 years. It will never be forgotten. As I go on with my life and look back on my career, when people ask me what the highlight was, it will be pretty easy to answer that question. Nothing could ever compare to being a Red Sox. Nothing.

Yours in Red Sox Nation,
Dave Roberts

# Introduction

When I first received this assignment I thought it would be easy enough; after all, 100 things Red Sox fans should know and do before they die is a fun, all-encompassing topic open to my interpretation. That's exactly what this book is—my interpretation of events and facts that I've either covered as a baseball reporter in parts of the past four decades or watched as a fan growing up in the Boston area.

What I have found is that fans and journalists look at the game in very different ways. As a fan the game is your passion, your hobby, that thing you do after school or work as a family; as a journalist it becomes not only your passion but also your livelihood. I was taught about objectivity in journalism school; I learned that there should certainly be no cheering in the press box. Once my career was under way, once I started a job as a reporter and sat down at the keyboard to write about the team I covered day in and day out, the fan in me had to be banished forever. It was the sacrifice I had to make to get into the profession, to cover the sport (baseball) and the team (the Red Sox) that I loved as a child.

When I was a kid, I loved Tony Conigliaro. I've often asked myself if I would have loved covering him as a reporter. What was he like to deal with from a reporter's point of view? I once asked longtime *Boston Globe* baseball writer Clif Keane to tell me about Tony C. Keane was never shy about telling the media everything. When he was about to give me an earful, I stopped him, saying, "You know, Clif, never mind. I don't really want to know. He was my boyhood hero, and my memories are my memories. I don't want them tainted." I was always Tony C. playing baseball in my backyard. Feet spread wide apart, bat back, hands high. "Long drive deep to left.... It's over the Green Monster...for a home run!"

Even though you probably never met them or knew them personally, as a child there was something about certain players that you just loved, whether it was the way they played, the personality they displayed on the field, or some other intangible. Journalists can't have that same kind of affection for individual athletes as I did for Tony C. when I was a kid. As a journalist, I see them differently. I experience them immediately after a win or right after a tough loss. I see them at their best and their worst. But what I also see up close and personal, and what I respect, is their God-given ability, their talent, their dedication, and their hard work. Those are things I get to see behind the scenes with professional baseball players, things that amaze me.

Because even we writers are human, there are those players we like more than others. Some are sources for news and stories. Some are just good guys that we happen to hit it off with. There are others that we have adversarial relationships with, even those we wish that we'd never met at all.

Which brings me to Roger Clemens. I thoroughly enjoyed covering his Red Sox career from 1984 to 1996. His 192 wins tie him with Cy Young for the all-time Red Sox lead, and it's doubtful that anyone will come close to breaking that record. He struck out 20 batters in a game twice over a 10-year span. Sadly, his career in Boston ended prematurely due to a contract dispute. In 2007 allegations of steroid use by Clemens came to light in the Mitchell Report, claims which Clemens vehemently denies.

In terms of his work ethic and what made him great, the Clemens I saw and knew during his Red Sox years was unmatched until Pedro Martinez came along. Clemens is a Red Sox legend who unfortunately won his championships with the Yankees, a fact that has made him a villain in the eyes of some Red Sox fans. My guess is that five years after he's done playing, when he's eligible, he will go into the Hall of Fame in Cooperstown wearing a Red Sox cap (if Hall of Fame voters like myself decide that he was a Hall of Famer even before the alleged steroid use, and that such abuses were so widespread in the "Steroid Era" that it's impossible to exclude all the players suspected of wrongdoing).

In this book I have tried to include key Red Sox people, events, and moments. I'll take you through the heartache of 1946, 1948, 1949, 1975, 1978, 1986, and 2003. I'll also briefly touch on the dominant Sox teams that won in the early 20$^{th}$ century—in 1903, 1912, 1915, 1916, and 1918—and the ones that won in the early 21$^{st}$ century, the 2004 and 2007 squads. There has obviously been a lot to cover in between as well—a lot of Teddy Ballgame, a lot of heartache. I'll write about the great players—Cy Young, Carl Yastrzemski, Roger Clemens, Pedro Martinez, Wade Boggs, Bobby Doerr, Ted Williams, Babe Ruth, David Ortiz, Manny Ramirez—as well as unexpected heroes like Dave Roberts, George Whiteman, Bernie Carbo, and Bill Mueller. I'll share weird and wonderful events like "the Fog" game in 1986, the 1953 team that scored 17 runs in one inning, and the squad that hit four consecutive home runs in 2007. With so much to cover, 100 snuck up on me very quickly.

I know some of my 100 will differ from those you might choose, and my view of those players and events that we agree on might also differ. I'm leaving out a ton of things. You would need to write a book the size of *War and Peace* to be able to fit in everything special about the Red Sox. In some cases I'm bringing my perspective to you as a fellow fan. In other instances, my perspective is that of a journalist. And, because few of us were around to see Cy Young or Smoky Joe Wood, in some places I've had to take the word of some of our finest baseball historians, writers like Glenn Stout and Richard A. Johnson, whose *Red Sox Century* was the best book ever compiled and written on the history of the Red Sox. I've also been helped out by the words of some of the great sportswriters from the Boston newspapers of the early 1900s—the great *Globe* writer Harold Kaese, for instance, a Spink Award winner who covered the eras of the 1940s, '50s, and '60s like no other.

I knew Ted Williams—a player who would have to be featured prominently in any book about the best of the Red Sox—only as a spring-training hitting instructor in Winter Haven, Florida, and later in his life at the various Red Sox and Jimmy Fund appearances he made. I never personally experienced his disdain for the Knights of the Keyboard (as we writers sometimes call ourselves). Having a familiarity with the players of that age, called "the Teammates" by writer David Halberstam, I think I would have enjoyed covering Bobby Doerr, Dom DiMaggio, and Johnny Pesky, whom I have known for almost 30 years.

There's no doubt I also have a soft spot for the Impossible Dream team of 1967. Even before '67 I loved watching Dick Radatz coming out of the bullpen, joined on the field by Yaz and Frankie Malzone. I loved watching Tommy Harper steal a base—we saw very little of the running game while I was growing up. But like most fans of my generation, the '67 team hooked me forever. Not just Conig and Jim Lonborg and Yaz, but Mike Andrews, Reggie Smith, Jose Santiago, Rico Petrocelli, Jerry Adair, Jose Tartabull, George "Boomer" Scott, Joe Foy, and Elston Howard as well.

Because of my affection for that team, I always thought Dick Williams was the greatest Red Sox manager—until I started covering Terry Francona, who has already won two championships. I didn't really know Williams until he began returning to Fenway for anniversary celebrations for the '67 team. I was in Nashville at Major League Baseball's winter meetings in November 2007 when Williams learned he had been voted into the Hall of Fame by the Veterans Committee.

While some Sox history has been either good or bad, sadly some has also been ugly. Let us never forget that the Boston Red Sox were a racist organization for a long time. They were the last team to integrate. They could have had Jackie Robinson, but they passed. They didn't employ an African American player until Pumpsie Green came up in 1959. This is a sad but undeniable part of their history.

Special Red Sox "things to do" are also included throughout this book. Fenway is obviously the place to go if you can get tickets, which has become a tough undertaking as the popularity of the team has grown. That's why one of the things I suggest is taking a road trip to a destination that usually doesn't sell out, such as Tampa Bay, Baltimore, or Toronto. Yes, sometimes it's easier to get a Red Sox ticket in Baltimore than it is in downtown Boston. You can also head for the minor league affiliates to watch the young Sox make their way up to the big leagues in places like Pawtucket, Rhode Island; Portland, Maine; Greenville, South Carolina; Lancaster, California; or Fort Myers, Florida. And please, sometime before you die, watch a Sox-Yankees game, whether it be in Boston or New York. Actually, go to one of each. This is the last season Yankee Stadium will be open, so what better time to plan ahead and get some tickets to the House that Ruth Built?

As you go through my 100 things, you'll probably think of a thousand things I left out. But that's okay, because we all have our own special memories. As a Red Sox fan, a journalist, and a historian, I myself have no shortage of those.

# 1 Forever Fenway

The unique qualities of Fenway Park have been written of often and eloquently. Many writers have lovingly described the Wall, the Triangle, the scoreboard, Pesky's Pole, etc. For me, it's the smell. I have no idea what the smell is—it's impossible to explain or describe. It could be almost 100 years of built-up crud for all I know, but next time you step into Fenway, take a whiff. You won't smell that anyplace else in America. It's not a bad smell or a good smell. It just smells like Fenway, like a slice of Americana. It smells like history and a lifetime of experiences. It smells like Boston baseball.

The players come and go, and even the memories fade, but the one enduring constant about the Red Sox is the ballpark. Fenway was built in 1912 in the "Fens" area of Boston, hence the name given to it by the original owner of the team, General Charles Taylor, who also owned *The Boston Globe* newspaper.

Generations of baseball fans have created lifelong memories there. Just as baby boomers remember the day John F. Kennedy was shot, New Englanders remember their first game at Fenway. Taking in your first Red Sox game is a rite of passage passed down from fathers to sons and now from fathers to daughters. It's guaranteed that neither the child nor the parent will ever forget.

The ballpark has undergone numerous changes inside and out over the years, but somehow the core of the edifice never seems to change. It's funny how people react to seeing it for the first time. In 1984, when 21-year-old Roger Clemens was driven to Fenway for his first taste of the major leagues by farm director Ed Kenney Jr., Clemens turned to Kenney and said, "This isn't Fenway. This is a warehouse!" Kenney had to convince the young flamethrower that

1

*A 1994 aerial view of Boston's Fenway Park, which opened on April 20, 1912, making it one of America's oldest ballparks.* Photo courtesy of AP/Wide World Photos.

this was indeed his new home—and it would continue to be his home for the next 13 seasons, until he departed for Toronto as a free agent following the 1996 season. Clemens certainly grew to love the ballpark: the setting, the environment, and the challenge of pitching there.

It's easy to see why tours of Fenway are becoming very popular. They're available year-round, and you can smell...er...*see* for yourself all of the unique nooks and crannies around the ballpark that often make fans wonder, "How did they do that?" But even those little unseen places—such as the inside of the scoreboard in left field— are rapidly changing and being updated.

The biggest changes to the park, other than the modern improvements made by the John Henry/Tom Werner/Larry

Lucchino ownership group, came when Thomas A. Yawkey owned the team. He bought the franchise in 1933 and rebuilt parts of the ballpark that had been damaged by a fire. The left-field seats were part of the fire; the old owners hadn't bothered to fix them because they ran out of money. Yawkey leveled off an even stranger phenomenon in left field: Duffy's Cliff, so named because left fielder Duffy Lewis did a great job playing the ball despite the 10-foot incline in left that had been designed to keep nonpaying fans from sneaking into the ballpark.

One of the things you'll learn on the tour is that the first game ever played at Fenway took place on April 9, 1912, when the Red Sox played Harvard in an exhibition game as part of an open house the team held to allow fans to see the new facility. There were snow flurries that day, and only about 3,000 fans were present to witness the Red Sox beat the Crimson 2–0. The first major league game played at Fenway—an 11-inning, 7–6 win over the New York Highlanders (yes, the team that would eventually become the Yankees)—took place on April 20 before 24,000 spectators. A number of fans actually stood in the field area to watch the game because some of the seating was not yet in place. Tris Speaker drove in Steve Yerkes for the winning run.

The ballpark originally had a capacity of 27,000, but after Yawkey poured some $1.5 million in improvements into it, the basic bowl of the park looked much as it does now, with a seating capacity in the mid-30,000s.

Yawkey was the one who rebuilt the 37'2" tall left-field wall with tin, replacing the original wooden structure. He also added the netting over the Green Monster to prevent balls from damaging buildings across the street. That 23½-foot netting was replaced by the Monster Seats in 2005. On April 26, 1912, Hugh Bradley, a reserve first baseman, became the first player to hit one over the Green Monster. It was one of only two homers hit by Bradley during his career.

Yawkey added skybox seats in 1946. By 1947 Fenway had lights. The many ads that adorned the wall around the ballpark—a staple of all the parks in those days—came down. Some 30 years later the Yawkeys added an electronic message board in center field.

One very dramatic change occurred in 1988, when construction began on a high-end club that came to be known as the "600 Club" (and is now the .406 Club) at the location of the old press box. The press box was kicked upstairs. This construction changed the wind currents at Fenway forever. What had been a home-run-friendly ballpark, with the wind often blowing out to left, now became a tough place to hit homers—a phenomenon first discovered by Sox Hall of Fame third baseman Wade Boggs, a career .369 hitter at Fenway, who had a penchant for hitting the left-center wall. During the 1989 season, after the new structure was built, he realized that it was suddenly harder to do that.

Fenway was like a modern palace early in its existence compared to the humble digs of Huntington Avenue Grounds, where the Boston Americans had played their games. Currently the site of Northeastern University, the stadium held only 11,500 fans.

Fenway played host to the World Series in 1912, 1914, 1918, 1946, 1967, 1975, 1986, 2004, and 2007. It has also seen many famous debuts, including that of Alex Rodriguez, who played his first major league game there on July 8, 1994, at the age of 19. Babe Ruth also played his first game there, on July 11, 1914. It was also the site of emotional events such as Ted Williams's final at-bat in 1960—a home run—as well as the 1961 All-Star Game and the Carl Yastrzemski farewell on October 2, 1983.

With so many notable features—including the new Monster Seats, the Tony C. seats in right field, and the red Ted Williams seat, which was installed to commemorate the longest home run ever hit at Fenway (502 feet on June 6, 1946)—Fenway remains the most unique ballpark in baseball. No other ballpark can offer the Green

Monster, the Triangle in right-center, Pesky's Pole in right field, the Fisk Pole in left field, the old-fashioned scoreboard, and the ladder in left-center.

And, of course, the smell.

# 2 Teddy Ballgame

The greatest Red Sox player ever was Ted Williams. There has yet to be a player who can unseat him from that throne.

It isn't that there have been no contenders. Manny Ramirez will be a Hall of Famer and should surpass Williams's 521 home runs. David Ortiz is considered one of the greatest clutch hitters in Sox history. Carl Yastrzemski had a long career and the greatest single season ever in 1967, when he won the Triple Crown. Wade Boggs is a Hall of Famer and one of the greatest pure hitters in baseball. Jimmie Foxx and Jim Rice both had huge years and were feared hitters.

But Williams was an event in and of himself, playing during an era (1939–1960) that—with the exception of the 1946 World Series, which the Red Sox lost in seven games to the St. Louis Cardinals, and the 1948 and 1949 teams, which both fell a little short—was fairly uneventful from a team point of view. He played in some potent lineups that were exciting to watch, but they never won the big one.

Williams, ever so gracious *after* his playing career, was by his own admission surly to the fans and the media during his playing days. There was the infamous spitting-at-the-fans incident that he never lived down; nor did he ever tip his cap in thanks for the ovations he received after home runs. He never came out for curtain calls. He eventually mellowed, but only well after he had left the field for the last time. In a one-on-one conversation with this reporter in the mid-1980s, Williams said of his relationship with the fans, "They were great fans and great to me considering that I didn't pay as much attention to them as I should have. I just wanted to play and not have to deal with any of it. I got along fine with a few of the media people, but not all of them. I didn't understand the constant need to write about everything I did or thought. I probably didn't handle it so good."

Asked about all he had accomplished throughout his career, he responded, "I just wish I could have enjoyed it more. I wish we had won a championship, because the fans deserved that, and the fellas I played with deserved it. Doerr, DiMaggio, Pesky, these guys played their hearts out. To get that far some of those years with nothing, I think that just left us with such an empty feeling." Williams has always said that his one regret was that he didn't get to stroke the winning home run at any point in the 1946 World Series.

Williams had so many incredible moments, but the most memorable one in my opinion is his All-Star Game heroics in 1941. Nowadays nothing that happens in the All-Star Game means much because the game has been so devalued. But back then the All-Star Game was a source of pride to both leagues as well as to the players involved. It was truly an honor to play in the game, and all the players wanted to do something dramatic.

Williams was only 22 years old. At the All-Star break he was hitting .405, so his presence in that potent American League lineup at Tiger Stadium was electric. Don't forget, the game also came during Joe DiMaggio's 56-game hitting streak; much of the attention was on DiMaggio, but Williams was hitting over .400. Can you imagine having two ballplayers going after such amazing feats in one season *and* having them both playing in the All-Star Game for the same team? It was DiMaggio beating out a double-play grounder that future Red Sox manager Billy Herman couldn't handle and that allowed Williams to come up to the plate with two out and two on against Chicago Cubs righty Claude Passeau. Williams was thrown a 2–1 slider that he said came up to him "as big as a balloon." He deposited it in the upper deck, sending the crowd into a frenzy. Those who were there would never forget the sight of the young, tall, skinny Williams hopping around the bases like a little boy, so excited about what he'd done. Even in our conversations later in his life, Williams never forgot the feeling of that moment.

Yet the rest of the '41 season was also something to behold. Williams went up and down but stayed pretty close to that .400 mark. He came to the last day of the season basically hitting .400, but rounded off it wound up at .3995. Williams was under such scrutiny from the Boston media that there was no way he could just sit out and preserve his .400. So he played both ends of a double-header at Philadelphia's Shibe Park and went 6-for-8, 4-for-5 in the first game and 2-for-3 in the second game.

Some 19 years later, at the age of 42, "the Splendid Splinter" treated his last at-bat like any other, despite being slightly thicker in the middle. He had received a two-minute standing ovation before he stepped up. In his final at-bat, in the eighth inning on September 28, 1960, against 21-year-old right-hander Jack Fisher of the Baltimore Orioles, Williams stroked home run number 521. He rounded the bases as the 10,454 fans on hand that day at Fenway roared.

So many Red Sox fans missed that moment. Can you imagine if that few people came to witness David Ortiz's last at-bat? Nevertheless, it was an emotional moment. The guy on deck, catcher Jim Pagliaroni, was so touched by the moment that he started to cry. Many years later Pagliaroni said, "You knew you'd just watched the greatest hitter ever go out like he was meant to go out." Williams ran hard around the bases and never looked up at the crowd yelling "We want Ted!" He just ran right into the dugout. In the ninth inning manager Pinky Higgins made Williams go out to take his position, but he soon sent Carroll Hardy out to replace him. One last time, Williams ran in from the outfield to the dugout. And there went the greatest hitter who ever lived.

# 3 Roberts Rules

Many Red Sox fans came to believe in the "Curse of the Bambino," a term aptly coined by my colleague and friend Dan Shaughnessy. Chants of "1918!" were heard everywhere—especially at Yankee Stadium, where Yankees fans constantly rubbed it in, reminding Boston of the date of its last World Series win. In 2004, what had really changed?

The Sox won the wild-card spot in the American League, took care of the Angels in the American League Division Series, and then faced the Yankees in the American League Championship Series. They were down 3–0 in the best-of-seven series and had just been absolutely throttled by the Yankees, 19–8, in Game 3. How demoralizing. Remember the Boston Massacre in 1978? This was heading down that path. So Game 4 was just a formality, wasn't it? Get your butt kicked by the Yankees, hear more about 1978 and Bucky Dent, 1918 and Babe Ruth, and Grady Little's decision to keep Pedro Martinez in during Game 7 of the 2003 ALCS—and then go home with your tail between your legs and wait for the next kick in the teeth. Right?

But then came this incredible turn of events—this fortuitous, if not downright gutsy, play by a guy who had joined the Red Sox on July 31 in a trade with the Los Angeles Dodgers.

To provide a little background, every day Dave Roberts has spent in a baseball uniform has been enjoyable for him. Although distracted by Giants teammate Barry Bonds's pursuit of the home-run record in the summer of 2007, he was willing to reminisce with this reporter about what might be the key moment in Red Sox history: that fateful October night when Roberts stole the show.

"It was just that moment I think that every player wishes for and hopes for and prays for. It was a moment that was just meant for me. The reason the Red Sox had acquired me from the Dodgers was for precisely that moment. I think you feel that. You kind of sense that. I knew I needed to do something dramatic, but I also knew I couldn't fail. If I was going to attempt it, I had to make it. So everything hinged on that play. You don't get to experience that very often in the course of your baseball career," Roberts said.

It was the bottom of the ninth, and the Sox were down 4–3 on the brink of elimination. It was actually even worse than that. The Sox were on the brink of being swept by the Yankees. Kevin Millar worked a walk against the greatest closer ever, Mariano Rivera. Out of the dugout came Roberts to pinch run for the slow-footed Millar. Bill Mueller, who had won the batting title the previous season, was at the plate focusing on Rivera.

Roberts carefully took his lead—a large one. He had been studying Rivera's move to first base on video almost every day of the series, knowing he might find himself in a situation of this magnitude. Roberts took off on Rivera's first pitch to Mueller. Yankees catcher Jorge Posada made a good, strong throw to Derek Jeter, who was covering second base. But it was too late. Roberts had done it. Mueller then drove in Roberts to tie the game. The Sox went on to win the game and then went on to win the next seven after that to take the pennant and the World Series against St. Louis.

While Roberts can't take credit for all four wins—nor did he even participate in the World Series—he *does* get credit for removing an 86-year stain on an organization's legacy. He gets credit for an inspirational play and an inspirational moment that Red Sox fans should never, ever forget.

"No matter where I go, people remind me of that play," Roberts said. "I didn't spend a lot of time in Boston, but the appreciation I receive all over the country from Red Sox fans and baseball fans is just overwhelming to me. It was an emotional night, but I'm always reminded of it, and that feels good. I've had the honor of experiencing Barry Bonds breaking the home-run record as a teammate of his in San Francisco, so I've truly been blessed in my career to be a part of some extraordinary situations. That is one I will never forget. It was the toughest steal of my career because of the moment, because I couldn't be out, and because there were millions of people who knew exactly what I was going to do."

# 4 The Thrill of Schill

Curt Schilling's sock was bloodied by the popping sutures in his right ankle as he pitched the Red Sox to a 4–2 win in Game 6 of the American League Championship Series in 2004 against the Yankees, tying the series at 3–3.

That moment was every bit as heroic as Dodgers outfielder Kirk Gibson hobbling around the bases after a Game 1 homer off Oakland's Dennis Eckersley in the 1988 World Series. It was every bit as dramatic as a gimpy-legged Willis Reed limping on the court at Madison Square Garden in the 1970 NBA Finals against the Lakers.

This was science at its best. Sox team physician Dr. William Morgan had performed a creative procedure on Schilling's dislocated tendon in his right ankle, suturing the tendon to the skin. Blood seeped through the sock on his right ankle early in the game, but Schilling hung in for 99 pitches, exiting with a 4–1 lead in the seventh.

It was an incredible long shot that Schilling would even be able to pitch that day and, if he did, he knew it would be a one-shot deal. Schilling held his cards close to his vest, leaving the sports world on tenterhooks almost up to game time. Would he be able to play? He warmed up on the side before the game. The plan was that if he felt his ankle could stand up to the pregame workout, he would pitch. There was also a less ambitious Plan B: for Schilling to perhaps face a couple of batters in relief. But that wasn't good enough for Schilling.

"There's no game tomorrow," he said. "It's all about right now. It can be done. I could do it." He convinced manager Terry Francona and pitching coach Dave Wallace to let him go out there. He did it again in Game 2 of the World Series despite having awoken almost unable to walk because his ankle was so stiff. Dr. Morgan again sprang into action and cut a suture, freeing movement in Schilling's ankle and allowing him to pitch six very good innings against the St. Louis Cardinals.

Schilling has had a storybook career. He's won three championships: 2001 with Arizona, when he and Randy Johnson formed an unbeatable one-two punch, and two more with Boston in 2004 and 2007. Schilling was drafted by the Red Sox in 1986 but was included in a blockbuster deal made by Sox general manager Lou Gorman in 1988 that sent Brady Anderson and Schilling to the Baltimore Orioles for veteran right-hander Mike Boddicker. Schilling returned to the Sox as a free agent prior to the 2004 season.

At 41 years old Schilling will start the 2008 season with 216 career wins and 146 losses. He's 11–2 in 19 postseason starts with a 2.23 ERA and 4–1 with a 2.06 ERA in the World Series. Without question he's one of the best postseason performers in the history of the game, which could be a major reason why he will certainly get Hall of Fame consideration.

It's not known whether '08 will be his last season, but in '07 Schilling, a three-time 20-game winner, though never a Cy Young winner, began to reinvent himself. Formerly a classic power pitcher—he threw 96–97 mph at the height of his career—he has now become a finesse pitcher who emphasizes off-speed pitches instead of relying on pure speed.

Besides a Cy Young, the other accomplishment that has eluded Schilling is a no-hitter. On June 7, 2007, in Oakland, he had that chance. If only he hadn't shaken off Jason Varitek. That's when Shannon Stewart stroked a single to right to end the no-hit bid. "I should have listened to Jason," said Schilling.

Schilling is a very opinionated person. He often states his case on his blog, 38pitches.com, which has become a popular site among Red Sox fans.

# 5 At Last

Anticlimactic? Well, sure it was. A four-game sweep of the St. Louis Cardinals in the 2004 World Series could never have lived up to the ALCS, in which the Sox came back from a 0–3 deficit to defeat the Yankees in four straight. But winning the '04 World Series finally ended the Sox's long streak of incredibly bad luck— 86 years to be exact. There were no teasers like 1986, when the Sox were one strike away before the ball went through Bill Buckner's legs in Game 6 of the World Series as the jaws of Red Sox Nation collectively dropped. No, this time the wait really and truly was over. When Keith Foulke picked up Edgar Renteria's grounder to the mound, ran toward first, and underhanded it to Doug Mientkievicz to complete a sweep of the St. Louis

Cardinals, a collective shout of "At last!" was heard throughout New England.

The Red Sox could very well have suffered a letdown after beating the Yankees. Instead the Sox roughed up their inferior National League foes. It was fitting that the team they beat should be the Cards. St. Louis had beaten the Sox in '46 and '67, both times in seven games. This was indeed payback. The Cardinals certainly didn't have anyone of Bob Gibson's stature on the mound—not with Chris Carpenter missing the Series with a sore shoulder. The Sox held the Cards to a .190 batting average in the Series.

Manny Ramirez was the Series MVP, hitting .412 with one homer and four RBIs over four games. Not much for words, Ramirez said afterward, "I think we learned a lot when we played against the Yankees [in the ALCS], because we lost the first three games. And today I was talking to some of the guys and I said, 'Hey, let's go. Don't let these guys breathe.' We know what happened against New York. We came back."

The Sox took a wild Game 1 at Fenway, winning 11–9 before 35,035 fans. Second baseman Mark Bellhorn broke the deadlock with a two-run homer that bounced off the Pesky Pole in the bottom of the eighth on a 1–2 slider by Cardinals reliever Julian Tavarez. Jason Varitek had reached with one out on an error by Renteria.

"This team had a lot of heart and character," said Bellhorn. "Somehow I think we had the confidence to come back." The Sox made four errors, including a couple of really bad plays by Ramirez in left field, and still won a very sloppy game. But that's what this '04 team was all about: overcoming things, sometimes even themselves. They were able to do it because of their potent lineup. David Ortiz stroked a three-run homer in the first, and Ramirez knocked in a pair of runs late in a game where the Sox led 7–2 at one point.

Schilling took Game 2, 6–2, in a courageous performance, pitching with a dislocated ankle tendon that had been temporarily stitched into place. He allowed just one run on four hits in six innings. He admitted afterward that when he woke up in the morning, "I wasn't going to pitch. I couldn't walk. I couldn't move." Dr. William Morgan, who proved to be one of the off-the-field heroes of the postseason, removed a suture, giving Schilling more mobility. The Sox survived three errors by third baseman Bill Mueller with clutch two-out hits from Varitek, Bellhorn, and Orlando Cabrera.

Martinez pitched what turned out to be his final game with the Red Sox in a dazzling Game 3 performance, going seven scoreless innings of three-hit ball for a 4–1 win. Ramirez knocked in the first two runs of the game with a homer and a single, and Nixon knocked in the third run to provide the bulk of the Sox offense. The Sox took advantage of two base-running gaffes, one of which was fairly routine, with Ramirez throwing out Larry Walker at the plate in the first inning. A more memorable blunder came in the third, courtesy of Cardinals right-hander and former Red Sox farmhand Jeff Suppan. Walker had grounded to Bellhorn at second base and the Sox infielder went to first to record the sure out, but Suppan found himself caught between third and home. Ortiz, normally a designated hitter but playing first base in the National League ballpark, took Bellhorn's throw and quickly threw down to Mueller at third, who applied the tag on the very embarrassed pitcher.

Derek Lowe, who won Game 4 along with Curt Schilling and Pedro Martinez, was superb. Relievers Bronson Arroyo, Alan Embree, and Keith Foulke all did their jobs as well. Johnny Damon hit a leadoff home run in another Game 4 highlight. Trot Nixon stroked a bases-loaded double in the third, and Lowe took care of the rest with seven strong innings.

These were truly the best of times for the Red Sox, who celebrated into the night at the old Busch Stadium while fans in Boston ran wild in the streets celebrating the end of their 86-year wait.

# 6 The Rivalry

Red Sox fans are raised to hate the Yankees, pure and simple. There is nothing good about pinstripes or anyone who has ever played for that organization. Ted was better than Joe D. Carlton Fisk was better than Thurman Munson. Big Papi is better than Mr. October himself, Reggie Jackson. Dave Roberts is better than Bucky Dent. Terry Francona is better than Joe Torre. Dick Radatz dominated Mickey Mantle. Catch my drift?

If you've never attended a Red Sox–Yankees regular-season game or postseason contest, make it one of your top priorities before you leave this Earth. Tickets aren't easy to come by, but the excitement, passion, and emotion at Fenway during those games is second to none. It's the biggest rivalry in sports. It's two super-power teams with the largest payrolls in baseball going head-to-head 18 or 19 times a year and sometimes in the postseason. The drama is off the charts.

Wearing Red Sox garb at Yankee Stadium or Yankees attire at Fenway Park can be harmful to your health, but friends have had fun with this over the years. I remember sitting in the Yankee Stadium auxiliary press box in right field during the 2003 playoffs observing a man wearing Red Sox garb, whose wife was sporting Yankees gear. The two argued through the entire game. It was funny to watch. After the Red Sox won, the wife turned to the husband and said, "You're sleeping on the couch!"

I once discussed this with Dave Roberts, hero of the '04 season after his amazing steal of second base in Game 4 of the ALCS. Roberts has been through the Dodgers-Giants rivalry from both sides. But when asked to compare Giants-Dodgers and Sox-Yankees, he said, "Absolutely no comparison. I wasn't in Boston very long, but when those two teams play during the regular season, it's a World Series atmosphere. It can be some meaningless game in April and it's like the biggest thing going."

There was certainly a time in the 1970s when these teams truly hated one another. There was no love lost between Fisk and Munson in particular when they engaged in a collision at home plate that erupted in a fistfight in 1973. Bill Lee had his moments with Graig Nettles, as when he accused the third baseman of separating his shoulder in a scrum. The Yankees got the Sox in 1949 on the final weekend of the season to win the pennant. They got them again in '78 in that Bucky Dent playoff game. They got the better of the Sox once more in 2003 when Grady Little left Pedro Martinez in too long. But the Sox finally got the Yankees in 2004, coming back from a 3–0 deficit in the ALCS against all odds to beat New York in four straight and take the series.

There's been so much crossover through the years. The Babe went to New York from Boston. Sparky Lyle went to New York for Danny Cater. Mike Easler was traded for Don Baylor. Mike Torrez came to Boston from New York. Luis Tiant went to New York. Wade Boggs signed with the Yankees as a free agent. Roger Clemens went to New York via Toronto. Johnny Damon signed with the Yankees. Heck, even Sox owner John Henry once held a limited partnership with the Yankees. And there are many other cases.

After winning the '04 title, Henry called for a kinder, gentler rivalry, hoping the relationship between the two teams would become more civil than it had been when the "Evil Empire" moniker was coined by Larry Lucchino the year before.

"I'd really like to see this Red Sox–Yankees thing go forward," Henry told *The Boston Globe* after the Sox won the World Series in '04. "I don't want to see this rivalry decline, but I would like to see some of the mean-spiritedness on both sides end. I'm not necessarily talking about just George [Steinbrenner] and myself, but I would include George and myself. At this point it would be nice to reduce the vitriol that occurs with the fans and management. It really doesn't happen to the players, but everyone surrounding the players. I would like to see that reduced."

The modern-day hard feelings began when the Yankees acquired Alex Rodriguez after a Red Sox–Rangers deal fell apart. Then came an ugly bullpen incident involving reliever Jeff Nelson and a Sox ground-crew employee that drew criticism from Yankees president Randy Levine concerning the way Sox management handled the situation. Next was the '03 incident in which Yankees coach Don Zimmer charged Pedro Martinez after Martinez had hit a Yankees batter with a pitch; Martinez tossed the Yankees' Zimmer to the ground, triggering a bench-clearing brawl. There was also an incident in which Alex Rodriguez tried to whack the ball out of Bronson Arroyo's glove during Game 6 of the 2004 ALCS.

Sox fans started the "Yankees Suck!" chants that have continued through the years. There are T-shirts with the expression that sell like hotcakes outside Fenway Park.

You can experience it from afar. Watch it on TV. Read about it in the newspaper or on the Internet. But until you've seen a Red Sox–Yankees game live, you haven't experienced the essence of what is the greatest rivalry in sports.

# 7 The Fisk-Carlton

I owe a long-overdue apology to a college professor for an early-morning class I missed in the fall of 1975 while attending Northeastern University. You see, there was Game 6 of the '75 World Series to take in, and when it didn't end until 12:34 AM, the chances of making that 8:00 AM class were, in a word, slim.

Actually, thank Carlton Fisk, a Bellows Falls, Vermont–born and New Hampshire–raised catcher extraordinaire, for at least ending the night (or morning) at a reasonable hour. It was his walk-off twelfth-inning homer—we've all seen the video millions of times: Fisk waving his arms, jumping up and down as he tried to guide his drive off Pat Darcy down the line to fair territory—that ended the night. The ball clanged off the foul pole. Ah, the power of body language! The spectators in the bleachers couldn't believe it. This was the type of history I couldn't learn in a classroom, anyway. Was it the energy he created by jumping up and down and willing it fair that pushed the ball into play? I buy it. The Sox won 7–6, staved off elimination, and lived to see Game 7.

Fisk called it, "the most emotional game I've ever played" and said, "I will never forget this as long as I live."

No one will.

Fisk, a 1972 American League rookie of the year, was a once-in-a-generation catching talent. He was drafted by the Red Sox in the winter before the Impossible Dream season in 1967. He could do it all—hit, run well, at least for a big guy (to which his nine triples in 1972 attest), and call a heck of a game. He handled a pitching staff as well as any backstop in the game. He caught more games than any catcher in history, with 2,226. He hit 376 home runs and played in 11 All-Star Games.

Fisk had a bitter departure from the Red Sox in the winter of 1980 when owners Haywood Sullivan and Buddy LeRoux failed to mail him a contract by the December 20 deadline, totally misreading the Basic Agreement. Fisk became a free agent and signed with the Chicago White Sox on March 18, 1981, at the age of 33. He played in Chicago until he was 45.

"I think every guy, kid, athlete who has grown up in New England fantasizes about playing for the Boston Red Sox in Fenway Park, wearing the Red Sox uniform, and I was fortunate enough to realize that fairy tale," Fisk told *The Boston Globe*. "A lot of fairy tales have been told, and in every one of them, there's a scary part, an unpleasant part, but they all culminate with happy endings."

Even though Fisk spent more seasons in Chicago (13) than he did Boston (11), he went into Cooperstown wearing a Red Sox cap after reconnecting with the Red Sox after many years away. He had

*Carlton Fisk hits a home run off the foul pole on October 21, 1975, during Game 6 of the 1975 World Series.*

his No. 27 retired by the Red Sox; the White Sox did the same with his No. 72.

Fisk was known for his unique and intense training regimen in Chicago, which kept him behind the backstop until he was 45 years old. He was a rugged, tough guy who had classic clashes with Yankees catcher Thurman Munson. The Fisk-Munson competition was the essence of the Red Sox–Yankees rivalry. Their classic confrontation on August 1, 1973, at Fenway in a 2–2 game in the top of the ninth inning—when Munson tried to score on Gene Michael's botched suicide-squeeze bunt attempt—will never be forgotten. Munson came at Fisk full-bore, triggering a fight at the plate and a bench-clearing brawl that lasted almost 10 minutes and resulted in both Fisk and Munson being ejected. Fisk also fought with Lou Piniella, the fiery Yankees outfielder, on May 20, 1976. It was a similar situation. Piniella crashed into Fisk trying to score on an Otto Velez single, triggering another brawl. A "satellite brawl" ensued moments later between Bill Lee and Graig Nettles, in which Lee separated his shoulder.

"We didn't like each other," said Fisk. "It was true rivalry where each team tried to kick each other's behind every time we played. It was intense, but it was fun. We wanted to win those games so badly. We looked forward to them and I think the fans loved them. We put on a good show."

# 8 You're Joshing

By the time the 2007 season had ended it was obvious who the best pitcher in the American League was: Josh Beckett. Though he did not win the Cy Young Award—losing to C.C. Sabathia based on regular-season voting—Beckett, a 20-game winner, was a savior and a dominator in the playoffs and the World Series.

The Sox were down 3–1 to the Cleveland Indians in the best-of-seven series for the American League pennant. The Indians had an incredible opportunity in front of them at Jacobs Field—they were one win away from the World Series. But they had to crack the biggest nut of all: Beckett. If ever the Red Sox needed a dominant performance from their ace, it was now. Getting one would ensure the series would return to Fenway.

As hoped, planned, and expected, Beckett sent the Indians into a three-game funk. He struck out 11 batters in absolutely overpowering fashion, seven on swings and four on looks. He retired 19 of the final 22 batters he faced. The looks on the faces of the Indians' hitters was one of sheer amazement. They never had a chance. Not one f*cking chance. In fact, the only run the Indians even mustered came on a double-play grounder. The Sox easily won the game 7–1, and back to Fenway the series went.

The Sox seemed to catch an emotional break when Paul Byrd, who had beaten Boston in Cleveland 7–3, was outed for use of human growth hormone in a *San Francisco Chronicle* story that broke right before game time for Game 6. This was hardly the news the Indians needed. They were already free-falling. They had botched their chance to put the Sox away in Cleveland, where Boston beat up 19-game winner Fausto Carmona thanks to a first-inning grand slam by J.D. Drew. Carmona was pummeled for seven runs in all in a 12–2 Sox win in which Curt Schilling again pitched very well.

When the Sox were down earlier in the week, Schilling had predicted that Daisuke Matsuzaka would pitch a fine game if the Series went to Game 7—and Dice-K would get his shot. Schilling had worked with the Japanese star on his fastball command during the week and had predicted that if Matsuzaka ever truly got control of his fastball, he could become a 25-game winner some year.

Dice-K pitched well. The Sox bats came alive and got to Jake Westbrook. In the end, the Sox just beat up on the poor Indians, winning the clinching game by an 11–2 score.

Beckett was voted the ALCS MVP. It wasn't the first time Beckett, only 27, had shown himself to be a postseason hero. In 2003 a 23-year-old Beckett shut down the Yankees in the World Series as the upstart Marlins defeated the Yanks in six games. Beckett won the clinching game and took the Series MVP honors.

# 9 Rocky Mountain High

For the second time in four years, a World Series victory over an inferior National League team came rather easily to the Red Sox. The Colorado Rockies, who were outscored 29–10, hadn't been so hapless leading up to the Series. In fact, the Rockies had been baseball's favorite Cinderella story, coming out of nowhere to capture the National League wild card and then winning 21 of 22 games to reach this meeting with the Red Sox. However, the Rockies had eight days off after their sweep of the Arizona Diamondbacks in the NLCS, and the rust showed over four games.

From a Red Sox fan's perspective, what you have to feel good about is Jon Lester's Game 4–winning performance. The young lefty from the Seattle area was diagnosed with lymphoma in August of the 2006 season. He underwent heavy doses of chemotherapy treatments and was cleared for spring training, though the Sox went easy on him, making sure he was ready at every step of the way. He didn't make his major league return until July 23 versus Cleveland (he went six innings and allowed only a two-run homer to Grady Sizemore in a 6–2 victory), and it was clear that the kid had really grown up and his strength was coming back. In the Series Lester went five and two-thirds innings and got the win in the 4–3 clinching game in which a Bobby Kielty eighth-inning home run made the difference.

"This is what you dream about," said Lester after the win, with champagne pouring and spraying at all angles over his brown hair. "I've dreamt about this since I was a little boy. To do it after all that's happened, I'm so grateful and so blessed. You do this and the first thing that enters your head is you want to do it again and again. I hope I get this opportunity again, but if I don't, I know this feeling right now is something I may never feel again."

What a feeling it was. It was exciting enough that the Red Sox had come back from a 3–1 deficit to the Indians in the ALCS, but they now appeared to be a team possessed. While the Rockies had this incredible karma and momentum working for them, the Sox, based on winning three straight against the Indians, came in with guns blazing.

Josh Beckett, the ALCS MVP, was terrific in leading Boston to a 13–1 win in Game 1 at Fenway on a sometimes wet night before 36,733 spectators. The 12-run spread was the biggest margin of victory ever in a World Series opener. Beckett struck out the first four Rockies hitters en route to nine for the night. Thirty of his first 32 pitches were fastballs. The Sox offense roped 17 hits, 16 of them coming in the first five innings. They sent 13 batters up in the fifth with nine consecutive batters reaching base. They struck for eight doubles.

It was complete and utter domination.

Game 2 was a 2–1 pitchers duel in which Boston's bullpen shone along with Curt Schilling. Hideki Okajima, the first Japanese pitcher to ever appear in a World Series game, retired all seven batters he faced, four with strikeouts. He relieved Schilling and held the status quo for closer Jonathan Papelbon, who picked Matt Holliday off first base to end the eighth inning and then shut the door on the Rockies in the ninth. Papelbon called it "the biggest out of my career."

The Sox didn't do much off young Rockies starter Ubaldo Jimenez. They got one in the fourth when Mike Lowell walked with one out. J.D. Drew lined a single to right, advancing Lowell to third; Drew then moved to second when right fielder Brad Hawpe unsuccessfully tried to nail Lowell heading for third. Jason Varitek brought Lowell home with a sacrifice fly.

With two outs and nobody on in the fifth, Jimenez walked David Ortiz, his fifth walk of the game. After Manny Ramirez singled through the left side of the infield, Lowell doubled over third baseman Garrett Atkins, scoring Ortiz to make it 2–1—all the Sox would need given their superb relief pitching.

Game 3 shifted to Denver. The Sox had a day to get used to the mile-high altitude, but it was no issue. It was the Red Sox who soared to a 10–5 win to take a commanding 3–0 lead in the Series. Rookies Jacoby Ellsbury and Dustin Pedroia pounded out seven hits between them. Ellsbury had four hits, becoming just the third rookie in history with four hits in a Series game. Daisuke Matsuzaka had himself quite a game—a two-run single in a six-run third inning, a great fielding play (capturing former Seibu Lions teammate Kaz Matzui off second base in the first inning after making a nice stab of Holliday's comebacker), and a very good outing on the mound. Dice-K had a three-hit shutout heading into the sixth inning but was replaced after walking Todd Helton and Atkins.

The Rockies pulled to within one run on Holliday's three-run homer off Okajima in the seventh; Papelbon then recorded the last four outs while the Sox offense tacked on four more runs.

In Game 4 Ellsbury, who started the season at Double A, proved to be the igniter. Leading off, he doubled on the second pitch from Aaron Cook into the left-field corner and then scored on an Ortiz single. Up 1–0 with Jon Lester looking pretty solid, the Sox added a run in the fifth on a Varitek single that knocked in Lowell, who had doubled. Lowell then homered in the seventh, ending Cook's night. Kielty homered in the eighth for what would prove to be the winning run after Okajima surrendered a two-run bomb to Garrett Atkins in the bottom of the eighth, making it a one-run game.

Papelbon, whose jig had captured the imagination of the country after he celebrated the division-clinching win and the AL pennant with some crazy dancing, wound up pumping his fist, throwing his hands in the air, and jumping into Varitek's arms after striking out Seth Smith with a 94 mph fastball to end the 2007 World Series.

# 10 The Best of Times

Your humble correspondent picked the Red Sox to win the American League East in a preseason preview at the end of March 2007. After a sweep of the Toronto Blue Jays in early May, I boldly wrote that nobody was going to catch the Red Sox. That brought on a flood of hate mail from Yankees fans. Hey, just stating an opinion.

The Red Sox led the division from April 18 on. They were in first place for 166 days. They held a 10-game lead after 40 games, and by July 5 they were 12 games up. This was all very significant to Boston fans. They hadn't been treated to an AL East title since Kevin Kennedy led the Sox to the crown in the strike-shortened 1995 season.

In the era of the wild card, winning the division isn't a grand accomplishment for a team as long as they make the playoffs—but for the Sox, there is some significance to beating the Yankees during the regular season for a change. The Yankees got off to a terrible start and were 14½ games behind Boston by May 29. They valiantly came back to close the gap. The closer they got, the more Yankees hate mail I received, but in the end the Sox prevailed by two games. Funny, but I received no mail acknowledging my correct prediction.

The Sox, who went 96–66, were a robust 51–30 at Fenway but an even more impressive 45–36 on the road (a .556 winning percentage). They dominated interleague play with a 12–6 mark despite losing two out of three to the Rockies, who they would later sweep in the World Series. They were 36–17 in games decided by five runs or more, and June was their only losing month (13–14). They never endured long losing streaks—their worst were three four-game losing streaks—and they didn't go on any huge runs, either, boasting only three five-game winning streaks.

Sox pitching was both consistent and excellent all year. New pitching coach John Farrell—who had been a farm director for the Cleveland Indians and who'd accepted the on-field position in Boston amid reports that he could be the heir apparent for the general manager's job in Cleveland—had a lot to do with it. But it was mostly the visible reality that the Sox had an emerging, young-yet-veteran staff led by 20-game winner Josh Beckett. They were second in the majors with a 3.87 team ERA. They had superb pitching performances along the way. Rookie Clay Buchholz, who was left off the postseason roster due to weakness in his shoulder, hurled a no-hitter against Baltimore on September 1, making a start for the injured Tim Wakefield. Veteran Curt Schilling came within one out of no-hitting the Oakland A's on June 7. Wakefield, a knuckleballer, won 17 games and had decisions in his first 26 starts before succumbing to shoulder issues late in the year that kept him off the divisional series and World Series rosters.

The Sox got big efforts out of their two Japanese pitching imports—Daisuke Matsuzaka, for whom the Red Sox won a posting bid of $51.111 million on November 14, 2006, and Hideki Okajima. Matsuzaka won 15 games and struck out 201 batters in 204⅔ innings. Hideki Okajima, a 31-year-old lefty reliever, became one of the top set-up men in the league, posting a 2.22 ERA in 66 appearances. His success was due mostly to the change-up Farrell taught him in spring training, which bullpen coach Gary Tuck called "the Okie-Dokie."

One of the biggest and best decisions made before the championship season even began was returning Jonathan Papelbon to the closer role after the young right-hander did some experimenting as a starter. The Red Sox were trying to avoid wear and tear on him after he'd suffered a scary subluxation of the right shoulder in a relief appearance on September 1, 2006, against the Toronto Blue Jays. The Sox decided to "manage" his innings and appearances, and the results were astounding: 37 saves, a .146 opponent batting average, and a strikeout rate of 12.96 whiffs per nine innings.

While there were a couple of questionable free-agent signings—the team saw 11 homers and 64 RBIs from right fielder J.D. Drew (signed for five years at $70 million) and a .197 first-half average from shortstop Julio Lugo (signed for four years at $36 million)—the Sox received a boost in the form of a tremendous year out of American League Rookie of the Year second baseman Dustin Pedroia, who overcame a .172 batting average as of May 1 to hit .317 on the season with a .380 on-base percentage. Pedroia was the victim of a good deal of bad-mouthing concerning his ability. Scouts from other teams often wondered aloud (albeit without attribution) what on Earth the Red Sox were thinking when they handed him the starting second-base job. But as one Sox minor league coach said, "Give him time. He'll grow on you." That he did.

The most consistent hitter start to finish was World Series MVP Mike Lowell, who hit a career-high .324 with 120 RBIs, both career bests. He absolutely destroyed at Fenway Park, hitting .373 with 14 homers and 73 RBIs while hitting 33 balls over or against the Green Monster with his uppercut stroke. Sox first baseman

Kevin Youkilis won a Gold Glove, committing no errors, and he also hit .288 with 16 homers and 83 RBIs.

David Ortiz did not come close to hitting 54 homers, as he had in 2006, but it didn't matter. He still managed to have a phenomenal season despite a balky right knee that often caused him pain and discomfort during the campaign. Ortiz, who hit 35 homers and knocked in 117 runs, hit .352 during the second half of the season. He hit .441 in his last 16 games with seven homers, eight doubles, and 19 RBIs and then continued that hot hitting into the postseason.

Manny Ramirez was not himself for most of the season, not producing the great numbers he'd been accustomed to. He then missed 24 games with an oblique strain, but he returned to the lineup to hit .389 over his last 18 at-bats, and that hot trend continued into the postseason, where he hit .348 with four homers and 16 RBIs.

And last but not least is the Captain, Jason Varitek, who continued to be a stalwart behind the plate, firmly guiding the Sox pitching staff through an excellent and sometimes dominant season.

# 11 Big Papi, David Ortiz

Red Sox fans have fallen head over heels in love with only a few players in history. David Ortiz might be one of the most beloved. Affectionately known as "Big Papi," his very name still makes former Minnesota general manager Terry Ryan cringe. That's because Ryan gave up on Ortiz, allowing him to become a free agent.

*David "Big Papi" Ortiz has blossomed as a player since moving from the Twins to the Red Sox. He is best known for the big hit, and in 2006 he broke the Red Sox single-season home-run record with 54.*

"Torii Hunter often reminds me," said Ryan, "that letting David go was really, really stupid."

When he was a Minnesota Twin, Ortiz was a platoon player and had not shown the ability that he has since displayed with Boston. In fact, it was a few changes in his stance, suggested by former Red Sox hitting coach Ron Jackson, that changed Ortiz forever. His clutch performances have since been off the charts. In '06 he hit 54 homers, breaking the single-season Red Sox record.

Ortiz is best known for the big hit. None was greater than the one he walloped in the '04 divisional series against the Angels, when he hit a walk-off homer in the tenth inning to complete a three-game Sox sweep. It was easy to see why Sox teammates were a little giddy afterward, and why Ortiz's head was soaked with every open bottle of champagne and every bucket of cold water in the Sox clubhouse. He stepped up against lefty Jarrod Washburn with one on and two outs. Washburn threw Ortiz a slider that hung up in the strike zone. He stroked it the other way to left, and the ball sailed over the Green Monster for an 8–6 win and a sweep of the Angels in the best-of-five division series.

At the time the hit had the feel of Carlton Fisk's classic 1975 World Series Game 6 walk-off, even though it was only the first round of the playoffs. It was a huge win because the Sox could have easily lost their momentum, having squandered a 6–1 lead when Vladimir Guerrero smacked a seventh-inning grand slam.

Ortiz had a few walk-offs in '06 and then struggled in '07 at the start of the year with knee, shoulder, and hamstring injuries. His homers went from 54 to 35 and his RBIs from 137 to 117, but he hit .332, some 45 points better, and his on-base percentage was a whopping .445. He was hitting .314 with 14 homers and 52 RBIs the first half of the season and finished up hitting .352 with 21 homers and 65 RBIs for the second half.

# 12 Manny Being Manny

John Hart, the general manager of the Cleveland Indians when they drafted Manny Ramirez in 1991, remembered, "He was kind of a different kid." Really? Never noticed.

Hart recalls that Ramirez had been late paying some bills during a stretch in his first season with the Indians and bill collectors were beginning to call the Indians' offices. Hart decided to get to the bottom of it. "What we found was, Manny hadn't cashed any of his paychecks for the season. We were about halfway through the year. They were all in envelopes in the glove compartment of his car. We asked him why and he just gave us that Manny shrug and said, 'I don't know,'" Hart recalled.

There are so many stories and so many episodes of Manny being Manny. The player even had a shirt made up with the "Manny Being Manny" mantra printed on it.

Ramirez was born in the Dominican Republic and spent his high school years in New York City's Washington Heights neighborhood at George Washington High School. He was a shortstop when Hart first saw him play, but the most striking quality of his game was his hitting—it was like nothing Hart had ever seen before. The Indians planned to draft him in the second round, but Hart's scouts predicted Ramirez would be long gone. So the Indians took him 13th overall, and they have no regrets.

Ramirez, a hitting savant, studies and practices his hitting ad nauseam. His ability to look at pitches going by before settling on an 0–2 pitch for a home run is legendary. Once during the '07 season David Ortiz kidded, "Manny, are you just playing around with the pitcher?"

Ramirez signed an eight-year, $160 million contract with the Red Sox in the winter of 2000. Leaving Cleveland was painful for him, especially since they had actually offered him more money, but the deal wasn't structured as well as Boston's. To say anyone can live up to that contract would be silly. But Ramirez, who was the 2004 World Series MVP and followed that with a .348 average with four homers and 16 RBIs in 14 postseason games in '07, has had a remarkable Red Sox career following his memorable time with the Indians.

Entering the 2008 season, Ramirez, without question a future Hall of Famer, will be 10 home runs shy of 500. His .593 slugging percentage is eighth all-time. His 1,604 RBIs are 28th and his 490 homers are 26th. He's hit 133 homers at Fenway Park and 131 at Jacobs Field. That's 250 homers in his home ballparks, with another 240 on the road. The '08 season will be his eighth in Boston, after the eight he spent with the Indians.

Ramirez has always been the subject of trade talk. The John Henry ownership group put him on waivers in an effort to rid itself of his contract. During the off-season in '03 they tried to deal him to the Texas Rangers—where, ironically, Hart had become the general manager—for Alex Rodriguez, but the deal fell through. Ramirez demanded trades in '04, '05, and '06, but the Red Sox were unable to ever get proper compensation in return for him. In '07 the reluctant Ramirez declared that he wanted to spend the rest of his career with the Red Sox. It looks like he'll get his wish.

# 13 The Man They Called Yaz

Ken Harrelson has often called Carl Yastrzemski "the Renaissance Man," because Yaz was responsible for a baseball renaissance in

New England. Dick Williams called Yaz's '67 season "the greatest season I ever saw a player have."

He was "the man they called Yaz." Popular Boston radio talk show host Jess Cain played the Carl Yastrzemski song—which was sung to the tune of "Hallelujah"—over and over on WHDH radio in 1967. "Carl Yastrzemski! Carl Yastrzemski! The man they call Yaz..." Cain belted over the airwaves. There was also Yaz Bread available in the stores for most of the '67 season. Some fans bought a few loaves and kept it frozen for years.

When his career began in 1961, the year after Ted Williams retired, Yaz was given the unenviable task of serving as Williams's replacement in left field. The son of a Bridgehampton, Long Island, potato farmer, Yaz had a very impressive minor league career, hitting .377 in Raleigh in the Carolina League before going on to play at Triple A Minneapolis in 1960. He was a very good young player who sported a funky batting stance with his hands cocked high, swinging the bat back and forth from the left side. He could hit for average and power, he could run, and he was a terrific defensive outfielder. He hit .321 in 1963 after he finally allowed himself to stop trying to become the next Ted Williams. "I was only 20 when I started and I wanted to be like Ted," admitted Yaz. "The pressure of replacing Ted Williams was there. As much as I tried to shed it, it took me a while to realize I wasn't going to be Ted and I needed to relax and just be me."

That seemed to happen in '67. He won the Triple Crown, which Williams had won twice. No player has won the Triple Crown since. Yaz hit .326 with 44 homers and 126 RBIs. He had an amazing .418 on-base percentage. Yaz would admit in a *Boston Globe* interview many years later, "I was really in a zone. You usually don't stay in it for 10 days, but I was in it for a month."

Yaz came close to replicating that season statistically in 1970 when he hit .329 with 40 homers and 102 RBIs. He had a whopping .452 on-base percentage. But the Sox, desperately trying to find that Impossible Dream feeling again, just didn't have it. The '70 Sox finished at 87–75.

Yaz, the favorite of owner Thomas Yawkey, seemed to win the clubhouse popularity contest over Tony Conigliaro, who had come back from his beaning in '67 to hit 36 homers and knock in 116 runs. Tony's brother Billy became the starting left fielder as Yaz moved to first base and became the team's designated hitter. He earned $160,000 in 1971, making him the highest-paid player in the league, but he often drew the wrath of fans, who booed him every time he made a key out.

He was one of the first major league players to undertake a rigorous off-season conditioning program, and without question he was the fittest player in the game.

Of course, no one can maintain that level of play forever. From 1971 to 1983, Yaz hit .300 only once. He made the final out of the 1978 playoff game against the Yankees and the final out of Game 7 of the 1975 World Series, when the Sox had a chance to win it. Yet he played in 3,308 games, more than any player in the American League. At the time he was the only player with more than 3,000 hits and more than 400 homers (3,419 hits and 452 homers). He knocked in 1,844 runs, won seven Gold Gloves, and played in 18 All-Star Games. He went into the Hall of Fame in 1989 on the first ballot.

# 14 The Impossible Dream

If you were a young Red Sox fan in 1967, after your mom tucked you in for the night you'd sneak the transistor radio into bed under your pillow for those late West Coast starts, listening to the mellow tones of Ned Martin.

Baseball was fun to follow in the mid-1960s, but let's face it: the Red Sox stunk. They lost 100 games in 1965 and finished in ninth place in '66; there was really no hope of this team ever being good. Jimmy "the Greek" Snyder set the odds of Boston winning the pennant before the '67 season at 100-to-1. And that's what it felt like. Oh, fans loved watching local favorite Tony Conigliaro and imposing closer Dick Radatz coming in to close games with that nasty look he gave hitters. But c'mon—the Sox weren't that big, even in Boston. This was a Celtics town with championship banners hanging from the rafters at Boston Garden and the parquet floor embedded in our minds.

Yet somehow, during that magical '67 season, something took hold. Young players like Tony C., George Scott, Joe Foy, Mike Andrews, Jim Lonborg, and Reggie Smith came up to the big-league team to join Carl Yastrzemski, the established star. Dick Williams, who had managed all of these guys at Triple A Toronto, was named the new manager. He had spunk. He made it clear from the outset that he was going to do things his way or the highway. Lovable guys like Jerry Adair, Jose Tartabull, and Ken Harrelson also made their own distinctive contributions.

So imagine what it was like, going from thinking of your hometown team as a perennial loser to experiencing a season that mesmerized you every single inning of every single game. If you're a baby boomer, this is the team that got you hooked on Red Sox baseball again. This was the birth of Red Sox Nation even before it was called that.

Many fans can still envision Rico Petrocelli catching that looping pop-up off Rich Rollins's bat in that last game of '67 on October 1 at Fenway to clinch the American League pennant in a 5–3 win over the Minnesota Twins. We can still see the TV clips of Sox players huddling around the radio in the tiny home clubhouse listening to the final innings of the Tigers-Angels game. When Tigers second baseman Dick McAuliffe grounded into a double play to end the game in a Tigers loss, Boston had won the pennant. The Sox players howled and celebrated.

That seemed like enough for us. The fact that the Sox lost the World Series in seven games to the St. Louis Cardinals and went face-to-face against the great Bob Gibson was great theater in and of itself. We didn't care that they lost. We were just so incredibly ecstatic that they got there.

Late in spring training in Winter Haven, Florida, Williams promised, "We'll win more than we lose." Ha! We all sighed collectively, wishing we could put our faith in his optimistic pledge. The Sox beat the White Sox at Fenway on Opening Day, 5–4, behind Lonborg before only 8,324 fans. That's how skeptical we were. The Sox drew only 3,607 spectators for the second game of the series.

But it soon became evident that something was different. Billy Rohr's flirtation with a no-hitter against the Yankees at Yankee Stadium, besting Whitey Ford in a 3–0 one-hitter, started the Impossible Dream rolling on April 14. If ESPN had been around, Yaz's tumbling catch to rob Tom Tresh of a base hit in the ninth inning would have been played over and over again. Ironically, the man who broke up the no-hitter with two outs in the ninth was Elston Howard, who would be acquired by the Red Sox in a deal on August 3.

The 22-year-old Tony C. set the town on fire when he stroked a two-run homer in the bottom of the eleventh in a June 15 contest against the White Sox to win the game, 2–1. The Sox were 31–31 on June 18, but Williams would soon start to make good on his prediction. From July 14 to July 23, the team embarked on a 10-game winning streak. When they returned from a road trip during the streak, an estimated 10,000 fans were waiting for them at Logan Airport. A frenzy began to spread amid Sox fans.

The Sox were pesky. They were fighters. They won close games and were appropriately called "the Cardiac Kids." During their winning streak they fought with the Yankees in a brawl that started when Yankees righty Thad Tillotson plunked Joe Foy and Jim Lonborg retaliated by throwing at Tillotson. The Sox constantly had to fight for respect. Crusty old manager Eddie Stanky of the White Sox openly dissed the Red Sox in mid-June; discussing Yaz, who was having an outstanding year, Stanky called him "an All-Star from the neck down." This was the type of stuff the players were dealing with, but they were able to ignore the talk.

Then tragedy struck. Conigliaro was hit in the eye by a Jack Hamilton fastball in the fourth inning of an August 18 game. The beloved young slugger was never the same. The Sox won the game 3–2, but the injury forced general manager Dick O'Connell to find a replacement for Tony C. He signed flamboyant Ken "the Hawk" Harrelson to a $150,000 contract for the remainder of the season.

On August 26 the Sox took first place following a 6–2 win over the White Sox that featured another Impossible Dream moment courtesy of Tartabull. In the first game of a doubleheader against the White Sox, with Boston leading 4–3, White Sox catcher Duane Josephson stroked a soft liner to right field in the ninth with Ken Berry at third base. Tartabull ran hard to make the catch and came up firing the ball to the plate. Not known for possessing a strong arm, Tartabull might as well have been Dwight Evans on this play. He made a perfect throw to Howard, who put a textbook block on the plate and tagged out a streaking Berry. The Sox held on to win and vaulted into first place. Many years later, Tartabull, who now works for the Atlanta Braves organization, said of the throw, "People still remind me of that play. I guess it's the play I was known for."

It was a year when Yaz won the Triple Crown and the MVP award, when Lonborg won 22 games and the Cy Young Award. The Sox went to the World Series against the hugely favored Cardinals, taking the competition to seven games, but they didn't stand a chance against the buzz saw that was Bob Gibson, who won three games.

"I think given what we'd gone through, we just felt like we were going to win the World Series, too," said second baseman Mike Andrews. But the loss didn't matter to us fans. The season was still magical. It made baseball important in Boston again.

# 15 The Throw-In

Mike Lowell was a throw-in, a salary dump by the Florida Marlins, who insisted that the Red Sox take on the two years and $18 million remaining on Lowell's contract if they wanted to turn a deal for Josh Beckett. The Sox agreed. In return they sent the Marlins phenom shortstop Hanley Ramirez, young right-hander Anibal Sanchez, and two young minor league relievers. It turned out to be one of those proverbial deals that helps both teams.

Lowell would become the 2007 World Series MVP, boasting a 6-for-15 performance with a homer and 4 RBIs. He had a career season in '07, batting .324 with 21 homers and 120 RBIs. From start to finish he was Boston's most consistent offensive performer. More important, he was one of the classiest Red Sox players to ever don a Sox uniform.

His story is so compelling.

Lowell sees the world through the lens of his Cuban and Puerto Rican heritage. He beat testicular cancer just short of his 25th birthday, four months into his marriage. He was an undersized kid (until he reached his early 20s) who maximized his talent to achieve a superb major league career.

When the Yankees drafted him in the 20th round in 1995 out of Florida International University, where his No. 15 was retired with a .353 career average, a move to third base threw him for a loop.

"It was a big adjustment for me. Third is so much more a reactionary position. The first step is key, so I needed to learn it. I was in the minors for two full seasons before I started feeling comfortable. It was actually a big motivation because I remember in '98, my first big-league camp, the Yankees had just signed Scott Brosius. He was coming off a subpar offensive year, but the Yankees were just going to stick him at ninth [in the lineup] and he'd play great defense for us. That's all we needed," Lowell recalled.

That's because the word on Lowell—which is hard to believe now—was that he was a good hitter but subpar defensively. He had made 56 errors in his first two seasons in the Yankees system, 21 at Triple A Columbus. He said some of the errors were because of bad field conditions and first basemen who couldn't scoop one-hop throws out of the dirt. But with Scott Brosius at third and the Yankees dynasty rolling, Lowell was traded to the Marlins in February of 1999 for three players of no consequence. He was going home, where his family could watch him play every day, something that had always been a dream for him.

Three weeks after the deal he was diagnosed with cancer.

"It totally changed me," admits Lowell. "I love baseball, love talking it and being around the game and talking shop with guys. When you're told you have cancer, your whole world stops. First thing I said to the doctor is 'When am I going to die?' It makes you realize what's really important. Sometimes you need those jolts of realism thrown at you. Maybe not that strong. Now I stress much less. I was 24 and married four months; that's something I don't wish upon anybody. It was tough for me physically and emotionally. But I had all my family there—a huge support group."

After beating the cancer, Lowell came back stronger than ever. He experienced lean years in Florida, but he was home.

"I think it was super convenient [playing for the Marlins]. That's what it was. It actually worked out great for me because

I've never felt pressure playing in front of my family. I actually prefer it because I don't have to make phone calls to say I did well or I did bad or whatever the case may be. [It was great] Living at home for seven years, and on top of that we had the same group of guys. We kept getting our butts whupped in 1999 and 2000 and 2001, and we kind of turned the corner. And then '03 was really a unique professional year for us. It was especially satisfying, particularly [for] the infield, because we got killed in those other years. And I think our infield became one of our strengths. We added Pudge [Rodriguez] and Juan Pierre. That was one of the most underrated aspects of that team: we had tremendous defense," he said.

He remembers the momentum mounting after the All-Star break—the excitement, winning close games. The Marlins fought to make the playoffs as the wild card, since the Braves could never be caught.

"I've often thought the best team doesn't always win in the playoffs—the hottest one does," said Lowell. "We were the hottest team. We clinched the wild card I think two days before the season ended. It was like a playoff run for us the last month. So I think we were in that playoff type mode. The series we played were unbelievable: a collision at home plate to end the Giants series; the craziness with the Cubs series and then going to Yankee Stadium. I felt like I had to go into emotional detox when it was over, but it was great," he said.

And his second one in '07 with Boston?

"Unbelievable. I've never felt so connected to a city, to the fans," he said. Lowell turned down a four-year, $50 million deal from the Philadelphia Phillies in November of 2007 to stay with Boston, with whom he has signed a three-year, $37.5 million deal.

# 16 Little Too Late

Manager Grady Little probably made the decision to stick with Pedro Martinez—no matter what—long before the fateful eighth inning of Game 7 of the 2003 American League Championship Series against the Yankees.

The Red Sox's top pitcher squandered a 5–2 lead and enabled the Yankees to take a 6–5 win over the Red Sox in 11 innings on Aaron Boone's walk-off homer against Tim Wakefield. "It bothers me that we lost the game," Little said at the time. "People are going to have opinions about certain decisions that lead to the results of the games. It just bothers me that all they can remember is the last game. That's what bothers me the most."

What bothered Sox ownership and a stunned fan base was that Little did nothing when it was clear to everyone except him that Martinez should have been taken out. He defended his decision, saying, "Pedro was throwing as well in the seventh and eighth innings as he had the whole game. He still had a lot of life left in his arm. He wanted to be out there and there's nobody I'd rather have out there." Little added, "My decision to leave him out there was no different than it has been the two years I've been here with Pedro. When he gets into a jam, he's the one I want out there trying to get out of that jam more than anyone else as long as he's got enough left in his arm."

The Yankees had strung together three consecutive hits by Derek Jeter, Bernie Williams, and Hideki Matsui. Most fans felt Martinez should have been pulled after Williams's hit. And if not then, definitely after Matsui's. But Little did nothing. And then came Jorge Posada's two-run tying double. It wasn't hit hard—in fact, it was just a blooper. But it looked so bad.

"It's easy to look back when it's done," catcher Jason Varitek said a day after the game. "But at the time, honestly, I didn't think there was any better guy's hands to leave it in than Petey's."

Little got a lot of support among his players, but it was clear that the ownership and the fans were completely against him. He had been a lame duck all season, but he still managed the Sox to quite a year. They had momentum and were two innings away from going to the World Series. Little wasn't the kind of manager who used statistical data to make his decisions, however, and that, in the end, was his downfall.

In a rather eerie postgame press conference, Little was asked only a few questions by the national media gathered in the bowels of Yankee Stadium. The reporters in attendance seemed to be in shock over what Little hadn't done. The next day he said, "I'm just thankful I'm the scapegoat instead of our players. I'm telling you the truth. I've thought about it a lot. I'm thankful that it's me instead of any one of them because if we don't win the World Series, which is the definition of winning, then somebody's got to be that man. I'm just glad it's me."

Little and Joe Torre, the Yankees' winning manager, played each other 26 times in '03; due to their late-game heroics, the Yankees held a 14–12 advantage over the Sox. Torre defended Little's decision, saying, "To have a manager be questioned about leaving the best pitcher in baseball in a ballgame when he's thrown 115, 120 pitches—it's tough."

No matter how many people came to Little's defense, the owners had made up their minds: Little was fired. A few weeks later Terry Francona came on board as the new manager of the Red Sox. He would lead them to two championships in four years. Little became manager of the Dodgers in 2006, but he resigned at the end of the 2007 season. Ironically enough, his replacement in L.A. is Torre.

# 17 Where Was Stape?

Some Red Sox fans may not want to know about the things in this section before they die—those of us who lived through them had a coronary at the time.

"The whole play was bizarre," Bill Buckner told *The Boston Globe* from his Idaho farm more than a decade later. "Marty Barrett was standing on second base to try to pick off Ray Knight. We had him picked off. I saw Marty move over to second, so I moved way over toward the hole. Normally, with Mookie [Wilson] you would play up with a runner on second base. You play a little deeper because you don't want the ball to go through. So then he dribbled the ball down the first-base line. The reason he would've beat it out had nothing to do with [Bob] Stanley getting over there. It's because I was so far out of position, trying to cover the hole over there. An infield hit still would've had Knight on third base. I had run up a long way, but I don't remember feeling like I was rushed.

"I didn't feel any kind of tension to catch the ground ball. Usually, when you miss a ground ball, it's because you look up. I didn't look up. The ball hit...I'm pretty sure the ball hit something...because the ball didn't go underneath my glove. It went to the right of my glove. It took a little bit of a funny hop, bounced to the right a little bit. It wasn't like, you know, you feel rushed and you look up. It took a funny hop. I mean, it's funny. It's funny. What do I chalk it up to? Fate. That's part of the game."

Buckner will always take the blame for the '86 World Series Game 6 loss, but of course there were things that happened that he couldn't control. With Wilson at the plate and the count at 2–2 with two outs in the tenth inning and Boston leading 5–4, it wasn't Buckner's fault that Stanley threw a wild pitch that bounced off catcher Rich Gedman's glove, scoring Kevin Mitchell from third base while Ray Knight went to second, bringing the score to 5–5.

Wilson fouled off a couple of pitches after that wild one, finally hitting the topper that Buckner couldn't handle on Stanley's 10th pitch. That sent Knight all the way around the bases to score the winning run as Mets players jumped high in the air and hugged and clapped, celebrating their improbable victory.

In my opinion as a Sox beat writer in 1986, there was no more courageous player in baseball that season than Buckner. His daily ritual when he woke up in the morning was remarkable. It would take him 15 to 20 minutes just to be able to put one leg in front of the other. He was practically crippled by a staph infection he had incurred in 1976 that really took a toll on his right ankle; Buckner had to massage his way into an upright position. Once he got going, he walked with a noticeable limp, and pain showed on his face. He'd get to the ballpark early in the afternoon to begin therapy on his ankles, ending by soaking them in a big bucket of ice water. You'd see him with wraps on his legs, knees, back, and shoulders. He looked liked a mummy. After games Buckner could usually be found in the whirlpool or back at his locker, again soaking his legs in ice.

Despite going through all of this, Buckner had a terrific '86 campaign with lots of big hits (batting .267 with 18 homers and 102 RBIs). He also had his best month over the final stretch of the season, hitting .315 with eight homers.

"Billy Buck was amazing that year," said Hall of Famer Wade Boggs. "He had more big hits than anyone on our team. He saved us like nobody else and he got very little credit for it. All he got credit for is what happened at the end."

Anticipating a Red Sox celebration, those of us reporting on the game had already gone down to the clubhouse area during the tenth inning. Heck, even the people on the field were anticipating a Red Sox championship.

"In the bottom of that inning we got two outs real quick," Boggs recalled. "I glanced over my left shoulder and saw 'Congratulations, World Champion Boston Red Sox' on the scoreboard. Harry Wendelstedt was the third-base umpire, and he asked me to flip him my cap when we won. He said he collected 'em from World Series games. Then [Gary] Carter hit the bloop over short. Then [Kevin] Mitchell hit the jammer over second. Everything started. Then all of a sudden we're walking off the field and I said, 'See you tomorrow night, Harry.'"

While the Mets celebrated their win—their entire bench jumping up and down at home plate—the champagne that had been wheeled from down the hall to the Sox locker room was quietly wheeled back into storage. The plastic covering that had been placed over the lockers came down slowly but surely as Sox players made their way back to the dank visiting locker room that, at this point, resembled a morgue.

It was the quietest postgame clubhouse I'd ever been in. For the longest time players sat there in stunned silence. Reporters didn't even dare to try to break the deafening silence by asking a question. But then Buckner himself decided he needed to get it over with, and he began answering questions about the play. And there, not far from Buckner's locker getting himself dressed, was Dave Stapleton, the one man who could have saved the world championship.

He had been Buckner's defensive replacement in late innings almost routinely for much of the season. Toward the end of games, Buckner, who was actually a very respectable defensive first baseman after years of playing in the outfield, would tend to stiffen up. Stapleton, who had been a starting second baseman and had played all around the infield in his super sub capacity, was not summoned into the role of defensive replacement that night by manager John McNamara—but he was waiting.

"I wanted to come in so badly and I just never got the nod," Stapleton said. "I guess Mac wanted Buck out there to celebrate."

Buckner made 14 errors at first base in '86. Stapleton had played 29 games at the position, handling 86 chances without errors. "I had a pretty good fielding average," Buckner recalled. "I don't think I missed a ground ball for three months or something like that. I was pretty steady on ground balls, but I did play a lot deeper than most first basemen. That's why I had so many assists, because I didn't want the ball to get through the infield."

He added, "Funny thing, the next year we went to Yankee Stadium and played the Yankees early in the year, and [Don] Mattingly hit a ground ball. Of course, being in New York, you're hearing all this shit. It was the exact same ball. And I did the exact same thing. That was one of the most embarrassing moments of my life. It was crazy. I mean, I was pretty good at ground balls."

# 18 Hero Hendu

Dave Henderson was a fun-loving, happy-go-lucky guy. He came to Boston in a waiver deal on August 19, 1986, along with Spike Owen, pitchers Mike Brown and Mike Trujillo, in exchange for shortstop Rey Quinones, and outfielder John Christensen.

Known as "Hendu," he didn't do much for the Sox over the next couple of months, hitting .196 with one homer and three RBIs in 36 games. But he made the most of his chance at postseason play in the middle of Game 5 of the American League Championship Series against California after starting center fielder Tony Armas sprained his ankle. The Sox were down 3–1 in the series, on the verge of elimination. Anaheim Stadium was the loudest ballpark I'd ever been in. My computer screen was flutter-

*David "Hendu" Henderson, here nailing a line drive in Game 6 of the 1986 World Series against the Mets, was a real asset to the Red Sox. Despite an outstanding World Series performance by Hendu, the Sox lost to the Mets in the tenth inning of Game 6.*

ing. Much of the story of how the Red Sox bowed out in five games had already been written.

Funny how things change. How heroes emerge. On his first chance in the outfield Hendu tried to make a play on a Bobby Grich drive to center and clumsily tipped the ball off the end of his glove over the fence. He made up for it, though. Henderson saved the season. After Don Baylor's two-run homer pulled the Sox to within a run, 5–4, Henderson drove a 2–2 Donnie Moore forkball out of the ballpark in the top of the ninth to give Boston the lead. This was a huge hit. After the Angels tied the game in the bottom of the inning, Henderson hit a sacrifice fly in the eleventh to score Baylor, giving Boston the winning run. The Series shifted to

Boston, where the Sox would win, going on to face the Mets in the 1986 World Series.

"I had waited my entire career for a moment like that," said Henderson. "When I played in Seattle, we'd be out of the race and watching the playoffs at home. It was a great moment for all of us because everyone had us dead."

Henderson's heroics didn't stop there. In Game 6 of the World Series versus the Mets, Henderson led off the tenth inning with a line-drive homer off Rick Aguilera on an 0–1 pitch hit down the left-field line off the "Newsday, It's a Hit" sign at Shea Stadium to give Boston a 4–3 lead that soon swelled to 5–3. "I thought it was like the closing chapter in my fairy-tale season," Henderson commented afterward. "I thought it was over right there." But it wasn't to be. Henderson even caught the second out of the bottom of the tenth, but he then watched helplessly as the Mets rallied when the ball went through Buckner's legs.

Up to that point, Henderson had hit .344 with three homers and nine RBIs in the postseason and .435 with two homers and five RBIs in the World Series.

After hitting just .234 for the Red Sox with eight homers in 1987, he was dealt to the San Francisco Giants for a player to be named later (Randy Kutcher) on September 1. He got back to the World Series three times with the Oakland A's, finally winning his World Series ring in 1989 when the A's defeated the San Francisco Giants. He batted .308 with two homers in that Series.

On a tragic note, Moore never got over the sting of Henderson's Game 5 ALCS homer. On July 18, 1989, he shot and killed himself in an apparent murder-suicide attempt. His wife survived the shooting. Moore's agent, David Pinter, admitted at the time that, "Ever since Henderson's home run, he [Moore] was extremely depressed. He blames himself for the Angels not going to the World Series."

# 19 Chicken Man

He didn't win his championship ring or his two Gold Gloves until he became a Yankee, but Wade Boggs joined Ted Williams and Carl Yastrzemski in Cooperstown as a Red Sox.

In 11 seasons with the Sox, Boggs, nicknamed "Chicken Man" by Jim Rice because he ate chicken every day of the baseball season, won five batting titles, stroked 200 hits for seven straight seasons, hit .361 or better four times, and hit .338 with the Red Sox (.328 for his career, the highest career average for any 20th-century third baseman), behind only Williams. He ended his career with 3,010 hits and was inducted into the Hall of Fame in 2005. Boggs was a self-made player who worked hard to become one of the best hitters and defensive third basemen in the game.

"I'd be the poster child for 'Moneyball.' I invented Moneyball," Boggs often kidded, referring to his on-base ability, which produced a career .415 on-base percentage.

For years the organization wondered if Boggs could make it. He didn't come up to the majors until 1982, spending six years in the Sox's minor league system. The Sox had Carney Lansford—who was coming off winning the American League batting title in 1981—at third base at the time. Boggs made the team as a utility infielder, seeing 49 games at first base, 44 at third, three as a designated hitter, and one in the outfield while hitting .349 in 338 at-bats.

He became one of the most colorful Red Sox players ever, making news with his very public affair with Margo Adams, the mistress who filed a palimony suit against him in 1988. Boggs referred to himself as a "sex addict" on Barbara Walters's television show.

Bill James rated Boggs the fourth-greatest third baseman of all time—behind Mike Schmidt, George Brett, and Eddie Mathews—in his book *The Bill James Historical Baseball Abstract*. Boggs's .415 on-base percentage is 26th all time.

His career was always tainted by whispers that he cared only about his statistics and that he wasn't a team player. Everyone thought Boggs had the strength to hit home runs, but that he wouldn't do it if it meant losing points off his batting average. Boggs always felt the rap was unfair and that by getting on base, he scored runs and helped the Red Sox win games.

Boggs had a bitter divorce with the Sox after the 1992 season, when he hit .259. Boggs felt the late Mrs. Jean Yawkey had promised him a five-year contract to end his career in Boston, but the Sox brass offered him only one year. He left as a free agent and signed a three-year deal with the Yankees, winning a World Championship with them in 1996. He also spent two years with his hometown Tampa Devil Rays.

"It's the highest honor any baseball player can receive," said Boggs of making the Hall of Fame. "There's no other silver bat, Gold Glove, or MVP that means more than this. When you look at 198 players in 103 years, that's a pretty elite club. It's an exclusive club. You've got to do quite a few things in order to get into this club. It's just not handed to everyone. The only time you can think about making it to the Hall of Fame is if you are close to 300 victories, 500 home runs, or 3,000 hits. The only time the Hall of Fame ever came into my mind was probably the time I was rounding first going into second when I hit my home run for my 3,000th hit. I thought, 'Well, there's my ticket. If anybody wants to vote for me for Cooperstown, then I've got the credentials to get in.' But getting in is another thing because there're a lot of great players who aren't in who have done so much for the game. It's astounding. [Bert] Blyleven. [Bruce] Sutter. You can keep going. And the way that I did it, by getting the third all-time amount of votes, just says that the writers respected the game that I played. That was the biggest thrill that I got, being recognized for the game that I played."

# 20 Rocket Launch

One of the best stories concerning the evening of April 29, 1986, when Clemens threw an amazing 20-strikeout game, was what happened to the late Larry Whiteside, the former baseball columnist and winner of the 2007 J.G. Spink Award; he also covered some basketball for *The Boston Globe*. That season I was covering the Red Sox for *The Patriot Ledger* of Quincy, Massachusetts, and Whiteside was there taking in the first couple of innings of the game. After two innings Roger Clemens had struck out five of the six Seattle Mariners he had so far faced. But given his dual role, Whiteside decided that he should probably opt for a ride down Storrow Drive to the Boston Garden, where the Larry Bird–era Celtics were taking on Atlanta in a playoff game.

As Mr. Whiteside drove down Storrow toward the Garden, reporters at the Garden had heard of Clemens's proficiency striking out batters that evening. They were thinking *no-hitter, perfect game,* or just *wow, a lot of strikeouts.* Camera crews were leaving the Garden and heading to Fenway. While Mr. Whiteside never made it back to Fenway, Clemens made history that night.

Clemens was just amazing that year. Not yet 24 years old, he had really come into his own with overpowering stuff and the unabashed confidence that the great ones have. He had a drop-dead curveball, a slider, and an overpowering fastball. He went 24–4 that season, winning the MVP and the Cy Young Award. And that night he turned on the heat and didn't let up. I remember first baseman Bill Buckner telling Al Nipper, "Roger's gonna strike out 18 tonight." Pretty close. The Mariners were ripe for this because they had struck out 166 times in their first 19 games.

Clemens fans had been putting up *K* cards along the back wall of the center-field bleachers that season. But as the night went on, with Clemens striking out eight straight at one point, the fans were running out of room; they also had to drum up a few more cards.

Ironically, one of the players Clemens struck out in the ninth inning was Mariners shortstop Spike Owen, who had been Clemens's teammate at the University of Texas; later that season Owen himself would be acquired by the Red Sox in a huge deal that also brought eventual playoff hero Dave Henderson aboard.

Clemens, still strong and pitching on pure adrenaline, looked into catcher Rich Gedman's mitt and fanned outfielder Phil Bradley on three pitches for number 20. Unbelievably, despite his amazing performance, Clemens was actually losing this game 1–0 until Dwight Evans lofted a three-run homer in the seventh to give Boston the margin of victory. Many years later Evans, recalling the night, said, "I just felt like I was part of history and something that will stick in my memory for the rest of my life. To have contributed to that, I think we all felt that was a special night."

Ten years later Clemens did it again. But this one meant more to him. By this point in his Sox career, the team's ownership and management didn't think Clemens had much left in the tank. He had gone through his worst stretch during the period between 1993 and 1996, with a 40–39 record, and was bothered by all sorts of nagging injuries to his shoulder, hamstrings, and groin.

The September 18, 1996, 20-strikeout game was not only his second of that variety, it was also his last Red Sox win. He ended his Red Sox career with 192 wins, tying Cy Young. The feat occurred at Tiger Stadium in a 4–0 shutout before only 8,779 spectators. The shutout was his 38th, which also tied Young for the all-time Sox record.

"He hit every target I put out there," recalled Red Sox catcher Bill Haselman. "I don't think I had to move the mitt more than three times the entire game. It was amazing to watch and be a part of. I've never experienced anything like it."

Reminding Clemens of his feat many years later while signing autographs for fans in Lexington, Kentucky, where he was preparing to join the Houston Astros in July of 2006, he said, "I always get reminded of that. The last thing on your mind is 20 punchouts. Doing it twice so far apart was out of this world. I just wish we could have won it all for the fans in '86, and I wish we could have made the playoffs in '96. We made a run at the end, but it wasn't good enough."

Clemens was always considered a workhorse who pitched through pain. His pitch counts often reached the 120s. But on that night in Detroit he threw 151 pitches and didn't walk a batter. Three times in the game he struck out the side. Travis Fryman struck out four times on 20 pitches. Tony Clark struck out three times on 20 pitches. Clark remembers, "I couldn't even see half the pitches."

While he couldn't convince Sox management to offer him a fair contract after the 1996 season, their American League East rivals the Toronto Blue Jays did. Clemens seemed very motivated to prove Sox general manager Dan Duquette wrong after Duquette said that Clemens was "in the twilight" of his career after a few tough seasons due to injuries.

If Clemens does not come back in 2008, he'll have received seven Cy Youngs, won 354 games, and struck out 4,672 batters.

Did he take steroids? He is named in the Mitchell Report, but as of this printing, Clemens has denied he ever took any performance-enhancing drugs.

# 21 The Curse of the Bambino

The phrase "The Curse of the Bambino," coined by *Boston Globe* columnist Dan Shaughnessy, perfectly characterized the plight of the Red Sox for so many years after Babe Ruth departed for the Yankees. The Babe was sold to the Yankees on January 5, 1920, after Ruth agreed to a contract with New York a year after the Red Sox won their last World Series. The popular version of the story is that owner Harry Frazee sold Babe for $125,000 in order to raise funds for his Broadway production of *No, No, Nannette*. But in reality, Frazee had just grown tired of Ruth's act. It was a bad move; Ruth was really coming into his own as a multidimensional player who could both pitch and hit, and his name would soon be synonymous with major league baseball itself.

Ruth made his Sox debut on July 11, 1914, at the age of 19 after coming to Boston from the International League's Baltimore Orioles along with right-handed pitcher Ernie Shore, catcher Ben Egan, and a lump sum of money. In an ironic twist, the three players were sold to the Red Sox because Orioles owner Jack Dunn couldn't compete at the gate due to the Terrapins of the Federal League also setting up shop in Baltimore. Should there perhaps have been an equally strong Curse of the Bambino aimed at the Orioles?

Ruth had already won 14 games in the International League before making his Sox debut on July 11 against the Cleveland Indians. He went into the seventh inning but gave up three runs after allowing the Indians only five hits over the first six innings. That's how it started, and it kept getting better and better.

From the beginning there were certainly signs that Ruth was going to be a great player. He had that something about him. He was hitting home runs at a time when nobody else was. He could run, hit, pitch, and throw.

Along with fellow pitcher Carl Mays, Ruth led the Sox with two wins in the 1918 World Series. But by 1919 Ruth was becoming more and more disenchanted with pitching and wanted to be a full-time hitter and outfielder. He also wanted a big pay raise. He had already signed on for $7,000, but at the urging of his adviser—yes, even then a star player's "advisers" could spell trouble for his relationship with the team—he demanded either $15,000 per year or a three-year, $30,000 deal. Frazee thought this both laughable and outrageous and made public comments that he would trade Ruth—who had threatened to quit baseball and become an actor—if he didn't show up for work. The two eventually managed to come to an agreement on the three-year deal.

According to *Red Sox Century* authors Glenn Stout and Richard A. Johnson, the Sox trained in Tampa that year alongside the New York Giants, and Ruth put on quite a show for the snowbirds. One prodigious shot (which may have become more and more exaggerated over time) had Ruth swatting a homer at between 500 and 600 feet; the spot where this ball supposedly landed is still marked by a plaque on the grounds of the University of Tampa.

By July 1919 team management gave in to Ruth's desires and curtailed the time he spent pitching—although they did not completely end his role on the mound—to allow him to spend more time playing in the field. Ruth's off-field issues became even more of a concern that season. He was often out at all hours of the night drinking and carousing, frequently breaking curfew. Ruth and manager Ed Barrow also clashed repeatedly, and Ruth openly campaigned for Jack Barry's return to managing the team. Aside from Ruth's troubles, the Sox weren't a very good team that year, never regaining the confidence and conviction they had had in 1918.

Ruth became an event at Fenway Park in 1919, much as Ted Williams would some 20 years later. He was hitting in the .320s by August and had already tied the American League record for homers (16) held by Socks Seybold; he would eventually wind up with 29. His superstar status was at an all-time high, yet Frazee still decided to offload him to the Yankees.

According to Stout and Johnson's account of the sale, there is no evidence that Frazee was in any financial difficulty, and in fact, *No, No Nannette* and Frazee's next Broadway show, *My Lady Friends*, were big hits. Frazee's true feelings about Ruth seemed to come out in a 1,500-word statement that he released to the media at the time of the sale. Here's a portion of it:

> Ruth is taking on weight tremendously.... He doesn't care to keep himself in shape.... He had floating cartilage in his knee, [which] may make him a cripple at any time.... New York is the only outfit in baseball that could have bought Ruth. Had they been willing to trade players, I would have preferred the exchange, [but] [Miller] Huggins would have had to wreck his ballclub.... I am willing to accept the verdict of baseballdom and I think that fair-minded parties of the sport will agree with me that Ruth could not remain in Boston under existing conditions.

Everyone knows the rest of the story. The Yankees received their drawing card. He hit 659 home runs for them and was part of the "Murderers Row" lineup that set all types of records and marks. Meanwhile, the Sox didn't win another World Series in the 20th century. Was it the Curse of the Bambino? How else can you explain it?

# 22 Pedro Mania

He never had the 20-strikeout games of Roger Clemens, nor the cache of Cy Young, but Pedro Martinez will go down as one of the greatest pitchers in Red Sox history. His 1999 season might be the best the team has ever seen.

Martinez went 23–4 with a 2.07 ERA. He struck out 313 batters and walked 37 in 213⅓ innings. He gave up only 160 hits and nine homers. He struck out 10 or more in 19 of his 29 starts. He struck out 15 or more batters six times. He had back-to-back 15-strikeout games on May 7 versus Anaheim and on May 12 versus Seattle. One of his most memorable games was on September 10 at Yankee Stadium, when he fanned 17 Yankees with no walks in a 3–1 Red Sox win over Andy Pettitte.

Martinez was a huge get for general manager Dan Duquette, who was looking to replace Roger Clemens as the team ace after Clemens was allowed to leave as a free agent following the 1996 season. Duquette had to put up with a whole year of ridicule before he found Clemens's replacement in the form of Martinez, who was no longer affordable to the small-market Montreal Expos. In a November 18 deal, Duquette sent Sox pitching prospect Carl Pavano and a player to be named later (Tony Armas Jr.) to the Expos in exchange for Martinez. The Sox then signed Martinez to a six-year, $75 million deal. They actually paid him for a seventh year when they picked up an option in his contract for an additional $17 million.

Martinez set Boston on fire with his tremendous pitching. The Latin community embraced him, and the ballpark was filled with Dominicans waving their flag proudly every time he pitched. Demand for Martinez's games was so high in the Latino community that the Sox decided to launch a Spanish-language radio network at that time. The Red Sox also picked up their scouting effort in the Dominican Republic and all over Latin America as a result of the Martinez buzz. *The Boston Globe* wrote game stories in Spanish every time he pitched.

Martinez's stuff was electric. He was dominant, some would argue even more so than Clemens had been. In seven seasons with the Sox he was 117–37 with a 2.52 ERA. His '99 and 2000 seasons were as good as they come. Old-timers said he was reminiscent of Sandy Koufax. His amazing six innings of no-hit relief in the 1999 ALCS against Cleveland is one of the most memorable performances in playoff history. He also threw seven shutout innings in Game 3 of the 2004 World Series.

Martinez certainly has had his controversial moments. He is known for being on his own schedule and often arrives late to the ballpark behind his teammates or skips pregame stretching. He became embroiled in a controversial episode during the 2003 ALCS when, after a series of hit batters, Yankees coach Don Zimmer charged him. Martinez shoved the back of Zimmer's head, pushing him to the ground.

He didn't care much for talk of the Curse of the Bambino, once vowing to "wake up the Bambino so I can drill him in the ass."

He was also the main character in manager Grady Little's controversial decision to keep Martinez on the mound during the eighth inning of Game 7 of the 2003 American League Championship Series after the Yankees had begun to hit him around. Martinez never received any blame for losing a 5–2 lead. All the blame went to Little, though Martinez tried his best to deflect the responsibility away from his manager. After the '04 Series Martinez, about to become a free agent, demanded a four-year deal, but the Red Sox were willing to offer him only three. The Sox's medical staff had serious concerns about how long Martinez's torn labrum would hold up before requiring surgery; they advised Larry Lucchino and Theo Epstein to offer him only three years.

After a long, drawn-out war of words, Martinez signed a four-year, $54 million deal with the New York Mets.

On the one hand, Martinez was true to his word when he said, "I'll never play for the Yankees," after the Series. He reiterated his desire to stay in Boston and even said in an interview before he signed with the Mets that he had told Lucchino, John Henry, and Theo Epstein that he had a four-year offer and that the Red Sox needed to step up. The Red Sox offered three years at $40.5 million with a $13.8 million option for a fourth year. But this was trumped by the Mets, who needed Martinez to revamp their team. The Sox stuck to their guns and let Martinez leave.

"We put our absolute best foot forward," said Epstein. "We've tried to keep Pedro Martinez in a way that makes sense for the ball-club. The team comes first, always. That said, he's been a great contributor. If the [offer] was not enough, we wish him the absolute best."

Martinez was 15–8 with a 2.82 ERA in '05 for the Mets, but in the '06 and '07 seasons he made only 28 combined starts. As the Red Sox predicted, Martinez's shoulder required major surgery. He did return to pitch for the Mets in September of '07 after missing the entire season, and he's expected to be at full strength in 2008, the final season of the deal that took him away from Boston.

With a 209–93 record and a .692 winning percentage, Martinez has assured himself a place in Cooperstown.

# 23 Feat of Clay

In the old days, if a guy pitched a no-hitter, he'd be back out there making a start four or five days later. Not so in the modern era, however. It's an age when innings pitched and pitch counts are rationed in the hopes that a young pitcher won't hurt his arm. That's why when 23-year-old Clay Buchholz made an emergency start for the injured Tim Wakefield on September 1, 2007, against the Baltimore Orioles and threw a 10–0 no-hitter in just his second major league start, he was immediately relegated to the bullpen for the rest of the season.

There was no outrage directed at general manager Theo Epstein, who has admitted that he and Terry Francona spoke twice in the seventh and eight innings of that game to determine how many pitches Buchholz would be allowed to throw (it turned out to be 115). If he'd reached the 120 mark, Epstein would have ordered Buchholz out of the game.

Buchholz, who grew up in Beaumont, Texas, was a much-ballyhooed Sox prospect in 2007. He breezed through Double A and Triple A and then came up to Boston with the September 1 call-ups and was pressed into action.

Basically, what Buchholz did that night at Fenway was move Billy Rohr's name aside. Rohr was a 21-year-old lefty who had a no-hitter going into the ninth inning against the Yankees on April 14, 1967. Rohr opposed the great Whitey Ford in that one, the same game in which Carl Yastrzemski made his immortal tumbling grab of a Tom Tresh liner, leading Sox broadcaster Ken Coleman to exclaim, "Yaz makes a tremendous catch!" With Buchholz on the mound in 2007, everyone wondered who would be the Elston Howard of the Orioles, the guy to break it up?

Earlier in the season, Curt Schilling had taken a no-hitter into the ninth against the Oakland A's only to have Shannon Stewart break it up with a clean single to right field. But Baltimore's Ellie Howard or Oakland's Shannon Stewart never emerged.

Buchholz's heart was thumping and his palms were sweating, but he managed to get a good enough grip on the ball and his emotions to retire the Orioles in order in the ninth. The fans went wild.

*Rookie Clay Buchholz achieved something most veteran pitchers never accomplish. After making an emergency start for the injured Tim Wakefield on September 1, 2007, the 23-year-old threw this no-hitter against the Baltimore Orioles.*

They stayed around the ballpark for as long as security would allow them that night. And it was a long time. It was an event. It was a night that everyone wanted to savor.

It's exciting enough when a guy like Buchholz or Rohr (who won the game 3–0) pitch lights out as young pitchers—but a no-hitter?

"I didn't find out I was pitching until the third inning of our game in Pawtucket," Buchholz told reporters after the game. "I had to gather up my stuff and get here. I didn't sleep very well."

The funny thing is that when the Sox made the decision to go with Buchholz, it was somewhat reluctantly, not only because of the 155-inning limit they had placed on his season but because he had struggled in his previous two starts at Triple A Pawtucket.

In his first major league start, on August 17 against the Los Angeles Angels of Anaheim, Buchholz knew he was going to make the start and then return to Triple A. Manager Terry Francona said before the start, "Doesn't matter if he throws a no-hitter, he's going back down."

And he did.

Buchholz had his own version of Yaz playing behind him. Second baseman Dustin Pedroia robbed Miguel Tejada of a base hit in the seventh inning when he roamed far toward the bag to make a diving, backhanded grab and then popped up quickly to gun Tejada down.

Buchholz ended the game with a called third strike on Nick Markakis on a 1–2 curveball; umpire Joe West followed the pitch into Jason Varitek's mitt and then rung up the kid's no-hitter, making history.

Because Buchholz had reached 140⅓ innings, the Red Sox made an organizational decision that his innings would be restricted for the rest of the season. He made one start of four and two-thirds innings and pitched out of the bullpen the remainder of the season; he was kept off the playoff roster when the Red Sox's medical staff determined he had a fatigued right shoulder.

# 24 Forever Young

You've got to admit, it's pretty impressive that Boston once had the pitcher for whom the award for pitching excellence is named: Cy Young. It's safe to say that Young was Boston's first big sports celebrity, joining the Boston Americans in 1901 as a 34-year-old right-hander who had played for the St. Louis Cardinals. Young jumped leagues, signing for $3,500. The story goes that Young didn't care for the heat and humidity of St. Louis in the summer and wanted to go someplace where it was a little cooler and where he could feel stronger during the dead of summer.

He won 192 games for Boston through 1908, which just so happens to be the exact total of wins Roger Clemens had for the Red Sox. Clemens was always fascinated by Young and read anything he could about the first Boston baseball superstar. It was always thought Clemens wanted to return to the Red Sox so he could break that tie, but it never happened.

In 1901, whether it was a case of global cooling or something else entirely, Young won the American League's pitching triple crown. He went 33–10 with a 1.62 ERA and 158 strikeouts for the Boston Americans. He pitched 371 innings that season. That's no misprint. For modern pitchers that's almost two seasons in one. He followed that up in 1902 with a 32–11 record.

According to the accounts given by Glenn Stout and Richard A. Johnson in *Red Sox Century*, Young was quite an attraction in those years at the old Huntington Avenue Grounds where the Americans played. Huge crowds gathered every time he pitched. It was akin to the excitement felt in the years when Pedro Martinez pitched at Fenway Park—there was just something special in the air.

Young pitched in Boston through the 1908 season. Into his forties by then, he was dealt to Cleveland, where he finished his career with an amazing and unbeatable 511 wins and 316 losses.

# 25 Meet the Yawkeys

According to firsthand accounts from players, front-office people, and folks who worked around the ballpark, Tom and Jean Yawkey were two owners who truly cared about the franchise. They paid their players well and cared about their personal lives. They also did all they could to win a championship, but they never did so in the nearly 70 years that they and the Yawkey Estate owned the team.

Tom Yawkey loved Ted Williams and Carl Yastrzemski. Yaz was like a son to Yawkey, and he paid both players the highest salaries in the game. Yawkey died in 1976. Jean, who grew up in Freeport, New York, was his second wife. He was married to his firs wife, Elise, when he bought the team in '33 for $1.2 million, but he divorced her in 1944 and married Jean a year later. Together they brought great players to Fenway, including Yaz, Williams, Bobby Doerr, Jimmie Foxx, Lefty Grove, Carlton Fisk, Wade Boggs, Fred Lynn, and Jim Rice.

But the one aspect of their stewardship that will forever be seen as a shameful Achilles' heel was that they were the last team in baseball to integrate. Yawkey had a chance to sign Jackie Robinson and passed. It was not until 1959 that he brought utility man Pumpsie Green on the field. For years Yawkey had to live with the whispers that he was a racist and that the Red Sox were a racist organization.

Yawkey's foster dad was once the owner of the Detroit Tigers, so Yawkey grew up loving baseball. When the Sox were up for sale he not only bought the team but also poured some $1.5 million into the ballpark, which needed refurbishing due to fires that had damaged areas of the ballpark; those spots had never been repaired. Yawkey, a Yale graduate, made his money in textiles, timber, and minerals and owned a lavish plantation in Georgetown, South Carolina.

Mrs. Yawkey, a former clothing-store model in New York City, reorganized the ownership structure and allowed Haywood Sullivan and Buddy LeRoux to buy into the team after Tom's death, but that caused more problems than anything. LeRoux attempted a takeover of the team in June 1983, but Yawkey and Haywood Sullivan prevailed in court. She later bought LeRoux out, and the Yawkey Estate, run by John Harrington, eventually bought Sullivan out as well.

Mrs. Yawkey was an extremely quiet, private person, but by Harrington's own admission she ran the organization. Harrington became Yawkey's voice, the front man for the organization. For many years she was the preeminent female owner in baseball. Cincinnati had Marge Schott, and San Diego had Joan Kroc, but Yawkey, given the magnitude of the franchise she owned, was the most powerful woman owner in baseball. In the years after her husband's death, Yawkey dealt with some major issues. Longtime general manager Dick O'Connell was fired in 1977. Fred Lynn was traded in 1981. Carlton Fisk and Rick Burleson departed as free agents the same year that Haywood Sullivan failed to mail the contracts out before the December 20 deadline. Mrs. Yawkey was on board with firing John McNamara in 1988 and bringing on Joe Morgan. She was also in favor of firing Morgan after the 1991 season, which proved to be a poor decision.

The closest a Yawkey came to winning a World Series was 1986, when the Sox were one strike away in Game 6 of the Series versus the Mets. Mrs. Yawkey died in 1992, but the Yawkey Estate, run by Harrington, continued to run the team until they sold it to the John Henry group in March 2002 for $600 million.

# 26 The Race Card

The two names that always come up when it comes to Boston's sordid history of racial discrimination are Pumpsie Green and Tommy Harper. Green became the first African American player on the Red Sox on July 21, 1959, while Harper, a player and later a coach, ripped the cover off one of the biggest Red Sox race scandals in 1985.

Green was not a remarkable player, but he was a pioneer on a team that was the last in baseball to integrate. Green called the moment "one of the most emotional and nerve-racking days of my life." He actually made his Sox debut on July 21 in Chicago as a pinch runner, but he played his first game at Fenway two weeks later at second base, where he helped turn a double play, taking a grounder and then turning the double-play with a strong throw to first baseman Pete Runnels.

"I ran off the field and into the dugout and got a bat," he told *The Boston Globe*. "I walked up to the plate and got a standing ovation from the crowd. It was heartwarming. I got lucky and hit a triple off the left-center fence."

Green became close to Ted Williams and warmed up with him before every game from the day he joined the team to the day Williams bid farewell to Boston on September 28, 1960.

"We had such a great relationship," Williams said. "We all understood the situation and what Pumpsie represented. We all knew he should have made the team from the start of spring training. I was just thrilled he got to experience being a major league ballplayer."

Extraordinarily, by 1985 there was still racial exclusion happening around the Red Sox organization. Harper blew the cover on the Winter Haven, Florida, Elks Club scandal; for years the club distributed dinner passes to white players but did not issue the passes to African American or Latino players. Harper's issue was never with the club but with the Red Sox organization for accepting the passes. This was one of the ugliest chapters in Red Sox history. It was bad enough that the Red Sox were the last team to employ an African American player. But this was 1985.

In one of the most important pieces ever written on the Boston Red Sox, *Boston Globe* columnist Michael Madden covered Harper's story. "I don't care that much what happens to me," Harper told Madden. "If they want to fire me or whatever…. But this has gone on too long with this ballclub. They're going to say to me that it's me stirring up trouble or it's you, but I'm not stirring up any trouble, because trouble has been right in front of their eyes for 15 years. And the Red Sox haven't done anything about this trouble, their trouble."

By '85 few players were being issued passes anyway, but Harper didn't find it funny when he found six Elks passes in his locker one day. He requested a meeting with team owner Haywood Sullivan in an attempt to end the practice once and for all. Sullivan had known about it for years but had never done anything. Madden had already gone to the Elks Club, where he had an angry exchange with some of the members who wondered why he was trying to stir up trouble. Madden quoted one man on why no black ballplayers had been allowed at the club: "Simple. Because we don't allow any niggers in here." And yes, this was 1985.

"It's the principle of the matter," Harper told Madden. "They still got those passes on team property, and they still hand them out, and some people still go there, even though the players don't go like they used to. The Red Sox should have cut their ties with this place a long time ago; to me, they're still condoning racism."

After the season Harper was fired. He filed—and won—a racial discrimination suit against the Red Sox. Today he is a consultant for the team; in 2007 he spent a few months working with rookie phenom Jacoby Ellsbury on his base stealing.

# 27 Doerr Number One

Over the years I've had the privilege of speaking to No. 1, Bobby Doerr, many times. Doerr is a nice, humble man who was content to be Ted Williams's teammate and table setter. But his number was retired for a reason. He was a great player in his own right, the best second baseman Boston ever had.

Johnny Pesky has often said to me, "You can look up his statistics and analyze them all you want, but they don't tell the story of the type of ballplayer Bobby Doerr was. He was brilliant. He did everything so well. He rarely ever made a mistake. He was just a born ballplayer."

That's why Doerr is in the Hall of Fame. That's why Williams used to refer to him as "the glue" of the team during the 14 years he spent in Boston from 1937 to 1951. Doerr had been in the league for two years before Williams came along, going 3-for-5 in his April 20, 1937, debut. Williams often called Doerr "the silent captain," saying, "He was all about baseball. He was all about what he could do to help us win a game. For all the people I feel badly that never won a World Series, Bobby was number one on my list because Bobby should have won one. I don't think I ever saw a player so devoted to the game. He was so underrated. He gave himself up a lot. He moved the runner over. If you were at a factory and they told you to build a perfect second baseman, I don't think you could put together a better one than Bobby Doerr." Along with Pesky and Dom DiMaggio, Williams and Doerr were dubbed "the Teammates" by author David Halberstam, who wrote a best-selling book about their special relationship.

In 1944 Doerr led the league in slugging percentage and finished second to Lou Boudreau in the batting race with a .325

average (his career average was .288). Although he never won a ring, at least he got to experience a pennant in 1946—the first one by a Red Sox team since 1918—and went on to play in the Series that same season. He hit for the cycle on May 13, 1947. There was a Bobby Doerr Day at Fenway on August 2, 1947, where he received a '47 Cadillac as the Sox won 2–1 thanks to a two-run homer by Ted Williams. He led the league in triples with 11 in 1950. He was a coach on the 1967 Impossible Dream team under Dick Williams, and his No. 1 was retired on May 21, 1988.

Doerr played in eight All-Star Games and 1,865 games in all. He once handled 414 chances with no errors, which was a record at the time. He was red hot in the '46 Series. He hit .409 with one homer and three RBIs. He recalled, "I was actually in a bad slump right toward the end of the season and then I tried to tinker with a few things and found my swing a few days before the Series. I think I got lucky, really. Sometimes you go a week or so when you're just not hitting the ball and then all of a sudden you go the other way. I've seen so many hitters who just get tired and worn out by the end of a season. But I think because it's the World Series, my adrenaline was flowing and even if I was tired, I didn't feel it."

Speaking of the 1946 Sox team, Babe Ruth once told the New York media, "Bobby Doerr—and not Ted Williams—was the number one player on that team. He rates the MVP of the league."

# 28 The 1999 All-Star Game in Boston

Al Forester, a Red Sox employee for more than 50 years, drove the golf cart that carried the 80-year-old Ted Williams around the ballpark during an incredibly moving ceremony before the 1999

All-Star Game at Fenway Park. Williams was announced as "the greatest hitter who ever lived" as the crowed roared. Forester, who had known Williams for years, was taken aback at how emotional Williams was that night. "It really got to him," Forester said. "He was really moved. While we were on the cart he commented that he couldn't believe the outpouring of affection for him. He was also cracking a few jokes, but he had a great time that night."

It was an amazing scene—31 of the greatest ballplayers of all time and All-Stars from the American and National Leagues gathered around Williams. Willie Mays, Stan Musial, Bob Feller, Cal Ripken Jr., and Bob Gibson were among those who stood around him, shaking his hand, sharing stories and comments. Everyone wanted to pose for a photo with "the Kid."

"It was like something out of *Field of Dreams*," said Jim Thome, who was on the American League roster as a Cleveland Indian. Mark McGwire and Tony Gwynn stood on either side of him. Carlton Fisk received as Williams threw out the first pitch of the All-Star Game while the crowd went wild. In a surreal scene, the players were so enthralled by being with Williams that they would not leave the field so the game could start. Gwynn commented, "You have an audience with the greatest hitter who ever lived who had the same San Diego background as I did, do you think I'm gonna get up and leave? That night brought goose bumps to everyone. You had the greatest players of all time all in that one area, hovering around Ted Williams. You knew this was something you'd never get to experience as long as you lived."

How could the players fail to be pumped up after that? Pedro Martinez watched the events as he warmed up in the bullpen. "This is probably more than I expected," said Martinez after being crowned the All-Star Game MVP. "I just wanted to be a part of it, have fun with it. I thought, seeing Ted Williams come in and the crowd going wild and the planes passing by, this one we'll hopefully all enjoy, the fans and me."

What did Martinez do to earn MVP honors? He struck out Barry Larkin, Larry Walker, and Sammy Sosa in the first inning and Mark McGwire and Jeff Bagwell in the second. The *Globe*'s Gordon Edes likened his performance to Giants hurler Carl Hubbell fanning Babe Ruth, Lou Gehrig, Jimmie Foxx, Al Simmons, and Joe Cronin in succession during the 1934 All-Star Game.

"When I saw Ted out there with tears on his face, I turned away because tears were starting to come to my eyes," said Rockies right fielder Larry Walker. "What an honor to be standing here with Ted Williams." Walker said the whole day was emotional for him.

Opposing Martinez that night was Philadelphia ace Curt Schilling, who was 13–4 at the All-Star break. Schilling allowed three singles in the bottom of the first inning to Kenny Lofton, Thome, and Ripken; walked Manny Ramirez; and left the first inning trailing 2–0. "Once I started to breathe after the third or fourth hitter, it was tough," Schilling said. "I mean, how do you follow what Martinez did? In his hometown, having arguably one of the best first halves in the history of the game, and he goes out and strikes out three above-average hitters. I said, 'That's nice. I have to follow that in the first.'"

# 29 The Red Seat

Section 42, row 37, seat 21—the Red Seat.

Patrons thinking about sitting in the bleachers at Fenway often hope that this special seat might just be theirs for the day.

Sox owner Haywood Sullivan had the seat painted red in 1984 after the Red Sox remeasured Ted Williams's famed blast of June 9, 1946; it was originally estimated at 450 feet but was actually

*The Red Seat (No. 21) at Fenway Park, pictured here, marks the 502-foot home run that Ted Williams hit on June 9, 1946. The remarkable blast by Williams remains the longest home run in Red Sox history.*

measured at 502 feet. It's the longest home run in Red Sox history. If you ever get a chance to sit there, you won't believe how far away it is from home plate. When you consider some of the hard-hit balls that are crushed and don't even come close to this distance, you realize that this ball was struck with incredible authority on the sweetest part of the bat at the optimum spot on the ball.

The *Globe*'s Dan Shaughnessy interviewed Williams on this topic many years later; describing the pitch from Detroit's Fred Hutchinson, Williams said, "He threw me a change-up and I saw it coming. I picked it up fast and I just whaled it." Boy, did he ever. It was a windy day, and the ball went over right fielder Pat Mullin's head and just kept on going, landing atop spectator Joseph A. Boucher's head in the first inning of the second game of a doubleheader. Boucher was wearing a straw hat, and the ball put a hole right through the top of it.

Boucher was a construction engineer from Albany, New York, and he took in Sox games every time he was in town. He rented an apartment on Commonwealth Avenue and worked at Park Square during the week. *Globe* baseball writer Harold Kaese spoke to Boucher after the hit. "How far must one sit to be safe in this park?" asked Boucher. "They say it bounced a dozen rows higher, but after it hit my head. I was no longer interested. I couldn't see the ball. Nobody could. The sun was right in our eyes. All we could do was duck. I'm glad I didn't stand up." Boucher was given medical attention at the ballpark, but he was okay, returning to his seat to watch the rest of the doubleheader.

"I just got the right trajectory," said Williams. "Jeez, it just kept going and going. In distance, it's probably as long as I ever hit one." So many of the modern sluggers have looked at the Red Seat and marveled, sometimes in disbelief. "No way, man," said David Ortiz, shaking his head. "How can anyone hit a ball that far?" Supposedly Ortiz hit one 502 feet at the Tokyo Dome in Japan during an All-Star Game, but he's never done it in the States. Manny Ramirez hit one over the light tower at Fenway that the public relations staff estimated at 501 feet, because there is no accurate measure of a ball hit over the Green Monster.

# 30 No, No, Nomo

Never seen a no-hitter? Not to worry—not many Sox fans have. The Red Sox haven't thrown many no-hitters in their history, but Hideo Nomo's gem on April 4, 2001, before 35,602 fans at Camden Yards was memorable for a few reasons. He struck out 11 Orioles and walked only three in his 3–0 win. The game ended a

36-year drought since a Red Sox pitcher had thrown a no-hitter (the last one was pitched by Dave Morehead in 1965, and before that it was Bill Monbouquette in Chicago in 1962). In addition, Nomo, the most celebrated Japanese pitcher of all time, was trying to get back on track after a subpar spring-training performance. It was his first start for the Red Sox.

Nomo was just the fourth pitcher at the time to throw no-hitters in both leagues (having pitched one with the Los Angeles Dodgers in 1996), joining Cy Young, Jim Bunning, and Nolan Ryan in that accomplishment. He was aided by a great play from second baseman Mike Lansing, who made a lunging, over-the-shoulder catch in short-center field to save the no-hitter.

Nomo, who spent only one season in Boston, was very humble after the win and said only, "I was very happy to have started my Boston career so well."

From 1900 to 1955, Boston had pitched 10 no-hitters. Cy Young and Dutch Leonard had two each. Young's first came on May 5, 1904, a 3–0 win by the Boston Americans over the Philadelphia A's [a perfect game]; the second was on June 3, 1908, in an 8–0 win over the New York Highlanders. Leonard's were on August 30, 1916, in a 4–0 win over the St. Louis Browns, and on June 3, 1918, with a 5–0 victory over the Detroit Tigers. Others were pitched by Jesse Tannehill, Bill Dinneen, Smoky Joe Wood, and Rube Foster. Babe Ruth and Ernie Shore combined on one in 1917. There was a 33-year gap between Howard Ehmke's 4–0 no-hitter over the A's on September 7, 1923, and Mel Parnell's 4–0 no-hitter over the Chicago White Sox on July 14, 1956.

Here's the rundown of Sox no-hitters since Parnell.

**Earl Wilson, June 26, 1962:** Wilson became the first African American pitcher in the American League to pitch a no-hitter. He did it against the California Angels, winning 2–0, in a game in which he homered before 14,002 fans at Fenway. Wilson's homer was a solo shot in the third inning off Angels lefty Bo Belinsky.

Wilson was aided by four outstanding defensive plays: a great catch by Carl Yastrzemski against the Wall on a ball hit by Joe Koppe; a nice catch by Frank Malzone near the dugout steps in the eighth; a great play by shortstop Eddie Bressoud on a soft liner hit by Billy Moran; and a game-ending grab by Gary Geiger of a Lee Thomas smash to center.

**Bill Monbouquette, August 1, 1962:** Monbouquette pitched the second Sox no-hitter in '62 with a 1–0 win over the Chicago White Sox at Comiskey Park before 17,185 spectators. He came out on top in this pitchers duel with Early Wynn when Lou Clinton stroked a two-out single that drove in catcher Jim Pagliaroni with the game's only run. Monbouquette, who improved to 9–10 with the win, walked White Sox third baseman Al Smith in the second inning and then retired 22 straight batters.

**Dave Morehead, September 16, 1965:** This is probably the most obscure game on the list, given that there was an announced paid attendance of only 1,247 (though some say there were no more than 500 people in the stands at Fenway that day). The Sox were on their way to 100 losses. It was also the day that general manager Pinky Higgins was fired and Dick O'Connell took over. Morehead allowed only a Rocky Colovito walk to lead off the second inning. He retired Vic Davalillio on a tapper back to the mound for the final out of a game that lasted only two hours. Lee Thomas homered and Dalton Jones knocked in Jim Gosger in the sixth inning for Boston's only two runs against Cleveland starter Luis Tiant. Morehead, only 22 years old at the time, went 10–18 in 1965 with a 4.06 ERA on a Sox team that went 62–100.

**Derek Lowe, April 27, 2002:** Derek Lowe pitched the first no-hitter at Fenway in 37 years. Nearly 3,000 starts were made at Fenway between Morehead's '65 no-hitter and Lowe's 10–0 win over Tampa Bay. One would think it would be difficult for a sinkerball pitcher to throw a no-hitter, but Lowe had the Devil Rays hitting the ball at people. The only base runner Lowe allowed was a third-inning walk to Brent Abernathy. He threw first-pitch strikes to 20 of 28 batters. Rickey Henderson ran under a Randy Winn fly that was heading toward the Wall in the first inning. In the fourth Trot Nixon ran down a Steve Cox liner toward the right-field wall. Henderson also ran down a liner toward the gap in left-center hit by Felix Escalona. Finally, Jason Tyner grounded a 2–2 pitch to Rey Sanchez at second base, who threw to Jose Offerman at first base for the final out.

# 31 Bucky Bleeping Dent

Maybe it was easy for Yankees owner George Steinbrenner to walk over to the Red Sox clubhouse on October 2, 1978, following a 5–4 playoff win at Fenway that gave the Yanks the American League East title. It was easy for him because the Yankees won.

Steinbrenner told the Red Sox, "It's a shame that this is not the World Series, that our series is not seven games, and when we're finished with each other, that the season isn't over. We are the two best teams in baseball. We said that on the field today. We won, but you didn't lose."

Clearly one of the greatest pennant races in major league history—featuring a dramatic collapse by the Red Sox, who had led the Yankees by 14½ games at one point—this epic contest came to a head when the two teams finished the 162-game regular-season schedule in a dead heat, 99–63.

Ron Guidry was pitching on fumes in this game after only three days' rest, giving the Sox a real shot at victory. His blazing fastball wasn't there. But Boston failed to take full advantage of all of their opportunities. The Sox went out to a 2–0 lead on Yaz's solo homer down the right-field line to lead off the second inning. Rice's RBI single in the sixth—after Rick Burleson doubled into the left-field corner and was bunted to third by Jerry Remy—provided the second run. Red Sox pitcher Mike Torrez was having a great day, striking out Thurman Munson three times; for a while he seemed to be outdueling 25-game winner Guidry.

Until the top of the seventh, that is.

Bucky Dent, the number nine hitter, became forever known as "Bucky Bleeping Dent" to Boston fans when he stroked a three-run homer into the netting in left field. It gave the Yankees a 3–2 lead and a complete momentum shift that won them the game and the chance to play the Kansas City Royals for the championship.

The top of the seventh started at Fenway before a packed house with Graig Nettles flying out to right field. Chris Chambliss and Roy White stroked back-to-back singles. Torrez then retired pinch-hitter Jim Spencer with a fly ball out to left field. There were two on and two out when Dent stepped to the plate. He'd gone 0-for-2 with a pair of fly-outs against Torrez and was also on a 0-for-13 slump. This seemed like a sure out, and nobody in the ballpark expected anything else from Dent that day. The frustrating part is that normally in that situation, a pinch-hitter would have been put in for Dent; however, because Willie Randolph was injured and Fred Stanley had to play second, there was no one else available.

Dent fouled Torrez's first pitch off his left foot. You even had to wonder whether Dent would be able to continue his at-bat, he was in so much pain.

*Globe* columnist Ernie Roberts quoted Torrez as saying, "Now I want to come in on him with a fastball low. It gets up a little. He's pulling away and hits it down the line. I don't think it's going to reach the wall. Then I think it may bounce off it. It goes over, a three-run homer, and I was so damned shocked. Bucky Dent. How can you explain that?"

We couldn't. Sox manager Don Zimmer, however, did have to explain why he yanked his pitcher after Torrez walked Mickey

Rivers in that inning. Zimmer brought in young Bob Stanley, who allowed Rivers to steal second base and then gave up an RBI double to Munson, who had been baffled by Torrez the entire game.

The Sox were snakebit by two defensive gems in right field by Lou Piniella. One came in the sixth inning against Fred Lynn, who tried to drive the ball to left field but hit a breaking ball to right instead. Somehow Piniella was positioned perfectly, toward the foul pole. And that wasn't even the best one. After the Sox had rallied for two runs in the eighth off Rich Gossage with RBI singles by Yaz and Fred Lynn, Gossage walked Rick Burleson with one out in the ninth in a 5–4 game. Remy then hit a line drive toward Piniella in right that the right fielder couldn't pick up because of the sun. It sure looked as though that ball might get by him after it hit the ground. If it had, Burleson certainly would have scored, but miraculously, Piniella kept the ball in front of him and fielded it. "I went to where I thought it would land," Piniella said. "I saw it when it hit and reacted." Burleson wound up at third with two outs, and Yaz ended the game with a foul pop-up to Graig Nettles at third for the final out.

Dent's homer wasn't even the game winner. It would take a Reggie Jackson lead-off homer in the eighth against Stanley—a blast into the center-field bleachers—to do that. Echoing Steinbrenner, Jackson told George Scott, "Both of us should be champions."

# 32 A World Series Odyssey

The Red Sox had collapsed in '74, were 11–20 in spring training in '75, and started 7–9 that April. How did Red Sox fans feel about their chances? Take a wild guess. Boston also lost 13 out of 20 in late June and early July. But somehow, they got their act together, and after winning 10 straight in mid-July, they were in it.

Darrell Johnson's team had an exciting offense led by the Gold Dust Twins, Fred Lynn and Jim Rice. Lynn took Rookie of the Year and MVP honors in the American League with a .331 average, 21 homers, and 105 RBIs. Luis Tiant and Rick Wise pitched well. They beat the Yankees three out of four in a key late-June series and outdueled the great Jim Palmer and the Orioles on September 16. They beat the O's by four and a half games for the American League East title with 95 wins. They were a team to be taken seriously. Underdogs in the playoffs, they swept three-time World Series champs the Oakland A's.

And so the stage was set for what many baseball fans still consider the greatest World Series ever played, Boston versus Cincinnati's Big Red Machine. Rice's broken wrist kept him out of the Series, representing a huge missing piece for the Sox. This was supposed to be a mismatch, but the Red Sox gave the Reds the Series of their life. In the end, Pete Rose would call it "the most exciting World Series ever played," and he was right.

The Red Sox shocked the Reds 6–0 in Game 1 on October 11 when Tiant mesmerized the potent Reds lineup with an array of off-speed pitches and curveballs to go along with his funky delivery. The Reds managed only five hits and never had a runner go beyond second base.

Umpires were watching Tiant's move to first base very closely because Reds manager Sparky Anderson had complained before the Series began that it might be illegal. Sure enough, umpire Nick Colosi made a balk call on Tiant in the fourth inning with Joe Morgan at first base; Colosi cited Tiant's "twitching knee" and advanced Morgan to second base. But that was to be the biggest threat from the Reds for the whole game.

Tiant battled Johnny Bench for 13 pitches before Bench fouled out. Tiant then struck out Mr. Clutch himself, Tony Perez, to wiggle out of the jam. In a scoreless game, Tiant started a seventh-inning rally against Reds starter Don Gullett with a single as the giddy crowd chanted "Looo-ie, Looo-ie!" A bunt attempt by Dwight Evans was fielded by Gullett, who threw toward second. The ball, however, struck Tiant and bounded into center field. After Denny Doyle singled to load the bases, Carl Yastrzemski's hit scored Tiant, who actually missed home plate and had to come back to touch it before the Reds could react. The Sox wound up with six runs. A two-run single by Rico Petrocelli highlighted the barrage.

The Sox had two excellent defensive plays in the game. Cecil Cooper robbed George Foster with a leaping catch of a liner in the second inning, and Yaz made an acrobatic diving catch of a Dave Concepcion liner in the seventh.

The next game was delayed 27 minutes by rain. It was a chilly October day, but Bill Lee, who seemed to be worn out by the end of the season, held on to a 2–1 lead into the ninth inning, when the Reds rallied to take a 3–2 lead. Johnson yanked Lee after Bench stroked a leadoff double. Reliever Dick Drago got the next two outs but couldn't retire Concepcion, who bounced a ground ball up the middle, scoring Bench with the tying run. Concepcion stole second base and scored on Ken Griffey's double to left-center. The Sox weren't able to come back, and the Series was tied at one game apiece.

The Series shifted to Riverfront Stadium on October 14. This was the scene of the infamous Larry Barnett call. With the score tied 5–5 in the tenth inning, the Reds got a runner on base when Cesar Geronimo singled against Sox reliever Jim Willoughby. Up came Ed Armbrister to pinch hit in an obvious bunt situation. Armbrister laid down the bunt in front of home plate, and catcher Carlton Fisk went after it. He collided with Armbrister while trying to field the ball and threw wildly over second base. Fisk and Johnson were screaming for an interference call, but none ever came.

"It was a simple collision," Barnett ruled. "It's interference only in the case of intent." Fisk lashed back, "I had to go after the ball like a [basketball] rebound in traffic. I'm an infielder. It was a ground ball. He was in my way. If that's not interference, then I don't know what f*cking is."

The Sox went on to lose the game as Geronimo went to third with Armbrister safe at first. Rose was walked intentionally; Morgan then singled over Lynn's head in center as the winning run scored. The Sox had come back from a 5–2 deficit on Bernie Carbo's seventh-inning pinch-hit homer and a ninth-inning two-run homer by Evans. Great comeback, but...

Down 2–1, the Sox notched the Series with Tiant returning to pitch another gutsy game—nine innings, 163 pitches. Tiant spotted the Reds a 2–0 lead, but the Sox came back in the fourth on a pair of singles by Fisk and Lynn followed by a two-run triple by Evans. He scored on Rick Burleson's double off embattled Reds starter Fred Norman, who was sent to the showers by Anderson in favor of Pedro Borbon. Bourbon allowed a single to Tiant; Perez then booted a Juan Beniquez grounder, and the fourth Sox run scored. Yaz knocked in the fifth run to make it 5–2. But the potent Reds came back to score twice in the bottom of the fourth. In the ninth, Lynn saved the game. With two on, Lynn made an incredible running catch toward the center-field fence to rob Bench of extra bases. Tiant then got Morgan to pop out to end the game.

Game 5 proved to be a revival for Perez and Gullett. Perez smacked two homers after going 0-for-15 in the Series, and the 24-year-old Gullett, the Game 1 loser, was in command all day. He was pitching a two-hitter heading into the ninth inning and leading 6–1 when the Sox strung together three hits and a run; Rawly Eastwick then came on to shut the door. Anderson predicted afterward, "If we play like this again, we will win the championship." The Sox weren't quite ready to concede. The Series shifted back to

Boston. But rain postponed the game three times. It was finally played on October 21, and it was worth the wait.

At 12:34 AM Fisk ended the game with a twelfth-inning walk-off homer off Reds reliever Pat Darcy; Fisk would forever after be a highlight-reel favorite due to his waving and jumping down the first-base line, willing the ball to stay fair. "This was the most emotional game I've ever played in. I will never forget this as long as I live," Fisk said.

The Reds were up 6–3 in the bottom of the eighth when Carbo produced a heart-stopping moment. Sox fans were in a panic at this point, facing elimination squarely in the face. Carbo blasted a three-run homer off Eastwick to tie the game. The teams also exchanged great defensive plays. Foster caught Lynn's fly ball to left and gunned down Doyle at the plate in the ninth. In the eleventh, Evans made a memorable catch, tracking down Morgan's drive and then turning and making a strong throw to Burleson, who was covering first to double-up Griffey.

Finally the Series came to a Game 7. It ended on Morgan's bloop single in the ninth off rookie Jim Burton to break up a 3–3 deadlock. Johnson was second-guessed for having a rookie pitching at such an important moment. "He didn't even hit it well," said Burton. "But the minute it went off his bat, it started to die. It was dying all the way."

The Sox had this one. They were up 3–0 through five innings. Lee—who allowed two runs in the sixth on a Perez homer after Rose broke up a double play and forced an errant throw by Denny Doyle—pitched very well but developed a blister in the seventh, and Rose singled in the tying run off Rogelio Moret.

# 33 The Gold Dust Twins

Jim Rice recalled, "Freddy [Lynn] and I just fed off each other. We both wanted to knock in the run and we challenged each other. It was a great situation—two young guys who were hungry and wanted to win. We came along at the right time. That was a good team and I think Freddy and I made it better."

There was no denying that. Can you imagine a farm system producing two players of that caliber at the same time?

Lynn, who had played at USC, was incredibly graceful in every area of his game. He could run effortlessly. He could go after balls in center field and track virtually everything down. He would often crash against the center-field wall to make a catch. He had the perfect left-handed swing and used Fenway to his advantage by going the other way.

Rice was a powerful man. He was clearly the strongest Red Sox player in years, hitting .364 in the American League Championship Series versus Oakland in 1975. He was not a great outfielder but an adequate one. He had power to the gaps, and he could stroke the ball to all fields. Hank Aaron watched him closely and felt that Rice, among all of the younger sluggers in the league, might be the one to break his home-run record. But Rice fell far short, with 382 homers, and is still trying to get into the Hall of Fame.

Who could ever forget Lynn's June 18 game versus Detroit, when he went 5-for-6 with three homers, 10 RBIs, and 16 total bases? Lynn almost hit a fourth homer in the game, but he legged out a triple instead.

Lynn's career was never consistent, though at times it was spectacular. In his second season a contract dispute intervened and he hit only 10 homers and drove in 65 runs. He was also injury prone. He did have another monster season in 1979, when he won the American League batting title with a .333 average, 39 homers, and 122 RBIs. But Lynn, who never felt comfortable in Boston, was traded to the California Angels in 1981 along with Steve Renko for Frank Tanana, Joe Rudi, and Jim Dorsey. He bounced around, spending the next 10 years going from California to Baltimore to Detroit and then San Diego. He never hit .300 again and never regained the form of his youth in Boston. He was a made-for-Fenway hitter and lamented after his playing days that he might have been a Hall of Famer had he stayed in Boston, where he hit .347 with a .420 on-base percentage and a .601 slugging percentage.

Ironically, Lynn wound up playing more years (17) than Rice (16).

While Lynn was known for his 1975 season, '75 wasn't too shabby for Rice, either. He hit .309 with 22 homers and 102 RBIs in a season that was cut short when Tigers right-hander Vern Ruhle broke Rice's left hand with a pitch in the top of the second inning at Tiger Stadium on September 21. Then in 1978 Rice had one of those memorable, off-the-charts seasons—a .315 batting average, 46 homers, 139 RBIs, a .600 slugging percentage, and 406 total bases, which at the time was the most since Stan Musial in 1948. He was the American League MVP. Rice, unable to play in the '75 Series, had to wait until 1986 before he got to play in the postseason; he hit .324 in '86 and was an MVP candidate, but he was surely overshadowed by Roger Clemens, who took Cy Young and MVP honors that season. He hit .161 with a pair of homers versus California and .333 with no homers or RBIs in the World Series versus the New York Mets.

Rice hit .298 in his distinguished career, with 382 homers and 1,451 RBIs. A .300 average and 400 homers might have made him a better bet to make the Hall. The 2008 vote seemed to be his best chance of getting in.

# 34 El Tiante

Before there was Roger Clemens or Pedro Martinez, there was Luis "El Tiante" Tiant. He was not just a starting pitcher—he was an event. In many ways he was held in the same regard and affection as David Ortiz some 30 years later. But in the mid-70s, El Tiante was one of the most popular Red Sox players of his generation. The Cuban-born right-hander, who smoked big old Havana cigars after a victory, often heard an entire ballpark chanting "Loo-ie! Loo-ie!" every time out.

His distinctive delivery—during which he turned his body completely to the outfield before turning back toward the plate and delivering the ball—was very difficult for hitters to pick up. He was short and a little on the pudgy side, and he spoke with a heavy accent. People loved him. The Sox acquired him in 1971 at a time when he had a hurt right shoulder; he had previously been a dominating pitcher for the Indians, winning 21 with a 1.60 ERA in 1968. He went from the Twins to the Braves before Sox GM Dick O'Connell signed him up.

Before the era of modern-day shoulder surgery, Tiant did his best to let his arm heal, but it was slow going. His performance, 1–7 in 1971, started to come around in 1972, and by 1973 he had won 20 games. He ripped off two more 20-win seasons in his Red Sox tenure and had some memorable moments with the Sox. He pitched a 5–0, two-hit shutout in his last game with Boston in the 162$^{nd}$ game of the regular season, versus Toronto, to force a tie with the Yankees in the division. Tiant also bested Jim Palmer, 2–0, in a huge September 16 game at Fenway in 1975 on a day when Tiant's Cuban parents were on hand. Fenway, packed to the brim, was electric. Tiant pitched a complete-game shutout as the place went wild.

There were so many other memorable games. On June 14, 1974, Tiant went 14⅓ innings in a duel with Nolan Ryan, losing the game in the bottom of the fifteenth when Denny Doyle, then playing for the Angels, drove in Mickey Rivers in a 4–3 loss. Ryan had come out of the game after 13 innings. In his next start five days later, Tiant went 10 innings in a 2–1 win. That was part of a stretch of games from May 9 to June 24 in which Tiant pitched 105⅓ innings over 11 starts with a 9–2 record. That's half a season's worth of innings for most modern-day pitchers. Fifteen times in his career Tiant threw more than nine innings in a game. Can you imagine a pitcher doing that today? The manager and pitching coach would both be fired and the pitcher would likely go on the disabled list.

Tiant won Game 1 of the 1975 World Series, 6–0, over the Reds. Performances like these were why he was known as Boston's big-game or "money" pitcher.

# 35 Rough!

Anyone who wins two championships in any sport has to be considered one of the great leaders. Bill "Rough" Carrigan holds the distinction of being the only Red Sox manager to have won back-to-back titles, leading the team to championships in 1915 and 1916.

Carrigan hailed from Lewiston, Maine, and was good enough to make it to the big leagues, spending all of his 10 seasons in the majors with the Red Sox. He was actually a player/manager when he supplanted Jake Stahl halfway through the 1913 season. He was good enough to finish in second place in 1914 before putting together a pair of championship seasons in 1915 and 1916.

*Bill "Rough" Carrigan, pictured here in 1939, managed the Red Sox to back-to-back championships in 1915 and 1916.* Photo courtesy of AP/Wide World Photos.

He was credited with nurturing Babe Ruth, who considered Carrigan a father figure. Carrigan gave him the obligatory pats on the back and, more important, the often-necessary kicks in the ass. For some 91 years, Carrigan held the distinction of being the only Sox manager to have won two world titles (until Terry Francona won his second in 2007).

What's amazing about Carrigan's story is that he walked away from baseball after two titles. He became a businessman and a banker. Obviously he got the itch to return, because he was named Red Sox manager again in 1927 when owner Bob Quinn, desperate to turn the fortunes of a dying organization, lured Carrigan out of retirement.

Carrigan was only 43 years old, but he'd been away from the game for some 11 years and it had changed quite a bit during that time. Given all the success he had in '15 and '16, when he won 101 and 91 games, respectively, his return was an abject failure. In fact, it was brutal. He finished in eighth place for three straight seasons from 1927 to 1929. In 1927 he went 51–103 and finished 59 games out of first. He followed that with a 57–96 season, ending up 43½ games back, and then a 58–96 season, 48 games back. The second Carrigan era then finally ended.

Carrigan really had nothing to hang his hat on despite the presence of excellent center fielder Ira Flagstead and Hall of Famer Red Ruffing on the team. But because the Sox were so bad, Ruffings's record from 1924 to 1930 was a dismal 39–96—not the best part of a career in which Ruffing won 273 games and earned himself a place in Cooperstown. His great years came with the Yankees, when he won 20 or more games for four consecutive years in the mid-1930s.

Carrigan died on July 8, 1969, at age 85, and was elected to the Red Sox Hall of Fame in 2004.

# 36 Franconian Proportions

In an era of multiple rounds of playoffs, winning two championships over a four-year stretch puts Terry Francona into an elite group of all-time Red Sox managers. Francona took over the team in 2004, replacing Grady Little, who was fired after keeping Pedro Martinez in the game too long in Game 7 of the 2003 American League Championship Series.

You have to understand how much pressure this was for Francona, replacing a man who had taken a team that deep into the playoffs and then wound up being fired. This meant one thing: for Francona's season to be considered a success, he had to get into the World Series. Well, that possibility looked awfully dubious with the Sox down 3–0 to the Yankees in the 2004 best-of-seven American League Championship Series, didn't it? Yet somehow, the calmness that is a staple of Francona's managing style came shining through when he tapped on Dave Roberts's shoulder to pinch run for Kevin Millar in the bottom of the ninth in a game that the Sox were losing by just one run. The move enabled the Sox to tie and eventually win the game. The Sox never lost again. They won four straight against the Yanks and four-time World Series champion Joe Torre and then swept the Tony LaRussa–led Cardinals in four straight.

Francona also got the Sox back to the playoffs in 2005, but they couldn't crack the buzz saw Chicago White Sox, who wound up winning the World Series. After an injury-plagued 2006, in which the Sox found themselves out of the playoffs, Francona guided the 2007 Red Sox to first place in the American League East for the first time since 1995. They beat out the Yankees by two games after spending 150 days of the season in first place.

It was a challenging season for Francona, who had to get two Japanese pitchers—Daisuke Matsuzaka and reliever Hideki Okajima—used to the American game. He also put his faith in rookie second baseman Dustin Pedroia, who captured Rookie of the Year honors. He dealt with a trying pair of free agents, J.D. Drew and Julio Lugo, neither of whom lived up to their billing. Francona also calmly guided the team back from a 3–1 deficit to the Cleveland Indians in the American League Championship Series.

Francona grew up as a baseball brat. He spent his childhood around ballparks, tagging along with his father, Tito Francona, who played for nine teams in his 15-year career. Terry was a number one draft pick (22nd overall) of the Montreal Expos in 1980 and played for five teams in his 10-year career, mostly as a part-time player. He later coached in several locations; his first (unsuccessful) tenure as a manager was for the Philadelphia Phillies, lasting four years (from 1997 to 2000). He never won more than 77 games there. In an odd footnote, Francona managed basketball superstar Michael Jordan in his attempt at playing baseball for the Birmingham Barons in 1994 and in the Arizona Fall League that same year.

Francona bought into the statistically oriented organizational approach implemented by Sox general manager Theo Epstein, and he also worked with two very good pitching coaches: Dave Wallace in '04 and John Farrell in '07. He is considered a players' manager, much like Little before him, and believes in resting his starting players more than most managers around the league. The philosophy paid off in both championship seasons, as the Sox always seemed refreshed in the postseason.

# 37 I Did It My Way

With a flattop hairdo and a butt-kicking style, 38-year-old Dick Williams, who had played for the Sox as a utility infielder in the mid-60s, was given the job as manager of the Sox to start the 1967 season. Williams had been managing in Toronto, the organization's Triple A affiliate, in 1966 and had run the show with the same stern style as he would in '67 with the big-league club.

Tom Yawkey gave Williams a one-year contract to see what he could do. With that in mind, Williams decided, "If I'm going down, I'm going down my way." That's exactly how he managed all season. He laid down strict ground rules with his young players. There were curfews, and he enforced them by performing bed checks. Nobody got away with anything. He challenged every player on the team to do better. He even fired off a bold prediction in late March during spring training, saying, "We'll win more than we lose." That was audacious considering the Sox were a ninth-place team in 1966—and there was little real hope the '67 Sox were going to be any different.

There was no question that in previous years that discipline had been lacking and the players had taken a laissez-faire approach. Williams changed that from the moment he took over the team during spring training. Workouts became longer. The team worked constantly on fundamentals. They did them over and over until they did them right. Williams didn't believe in working for a few hours and then going to play golf. He believed in making your baseball skills better.

Williams knew this wouldn't be a popular approach. But he didn't care. "I was very strict with them and they didn't like it. I think when they started to realize I was for real and that we got results, they bought into it. I never thought that players had to like me. I just thought they needed to play for me."

Reggie Smith, a young player on the team, said of Williams at a gathering at Fenway in 2007, "He taught me how to play the game the right way. It wasn't pleasant at times, and I could remember cursing him under my breath. But when you're a kid and this is what you come into baseball with, you learn to do things the right way. I carried that throughout my professional career. I have thanked Dick many times."

No doubt Williams got the most out of Triple Crown winner Carl Yastrzemski. Jim Lonborg came into his own under Williams and won the Cy Young with 22 wins. Williams lit a fire under Tony Conigliaro, a player he didn't care for until Tony C's tragic beaning on August 18 ended his season. Williams also had a knack for putting the right people in the right places. Utility man Jerry Adair was one of Williams's favorites; he moved Adair around and got great results. Norm Siebern was another guy off the bench in whom Williams showed faith. On August 19 in a key game against the Angels with the bases loaded, Siebern—hitting under .200 at the time—came up to pinch hit and stroked a bases-clearing triple in a game the Sox won 12–11.

Williams could certainly be grating on his players. His act would never go over in the modern game, where players are disciplined behind the scenes. Williams was never afraid to chastise a player in the press. But he got away with it back then because it was a young team and they feared him. "They didn't mind taking the World Series paycheck," Williams said later.

Williams signed a three-year deal in 1968, but he wouldn't get the chance to see it through.

In '68 Lonborg missed half the season after he tore up his knee in a skiing accident in Lake Tahoe; when he returned, he went 6–10 with a 4.29 ERA. George Scott fell to .171. Jose Santiago hurt his arm and didn't pitch. Yaz might have won the batting title, but he did it with the lowest average in history, .301. "Hawk" Harrelson became popular in '68, with 35 homers and 109 RBIs, leading the American League in both categories, but the Sox finished fourth, 86–76.

In '69 came expansion, and with it the major leagues underwent major rule changes. The mound was lowered five inches, and the strike zone was changed. New franchises in Seattle, Kansas City, San Diego, and Montreal entered the majors. Williams was still a taskmaster, once pulling Yaz from a game when he didn't run out a grounder on a tapper back to the pitcher. Williams also dressed down his superstar in front of the team. Yaz was a personal favorite of Tom Yawkey, and this move didn't go over well with the owner.

Williams was fired on September 23 by general manager Dick O'Connell, who was ordered by Mr. Yawkey to change the staff; Coach Eddie Popowski finished out the season in his place. But Williams's run was far from over; he reinvented himself with the Oakland A's in the early 1970s, finishing first three times and winning two World Series.

He was voted into the Hall of Fame by the Veterans Committee in 2007.

# 38 Mr. Red Sox

If you wonder what the Red Sox would be like without Fenway Park, then in the same breath you have to wonder what the team would be like without Johnny Pesky. He is Mr. Red Sox. He's at the ballpark for every home game. He's as much of an institution as the Red Sox themselves or the Pesky Pole down the right-field line that was named after him. For years I have advocated that his No. 6 be

*Johnny Pesky salutes the crowd after blowing out the candles on his birthday cake at Fenway Park on September 27, 2007. Known as "Mr. Red Sox," Pesky is present at every Red Sox home game.*

retired simply because of the unique nature of the many hats he's worn for the Red Sox.

Pesky grew up in Portland, Oregon, and decided against taking a little more money to sign with the St. Louis Cardinals, agreeing to a $500 contract with the Boston Red Sox on the advice of his mother. It's a move he's never regretted. The year was 1939. It is now 2008 and Pesky is still wearing the Red Sox uniform.

He was probably not as famous as his "teammates" Ted Williams, Bobby Doerr, and Dom DiMaggio, but Pesky's shelf life with Boston has been far more lasting. He's been a player, a coach, a manager, a broadcaster, a special assistant, an ambassador, and in general just a great human being. He dresses in his uniform before games and goes out to offer his expertise to anyone who might listen or need his advice. He used to sit in the dugout during games, but in 2004 Major League Baseball reduced the number of uniformed personnel that are allowed in the dugout, and by 2007 Pesky could no longer be there.

Pesky hit .331 as a rookie with the Red Sox in 1942, and then he left to fulfill his military obligations for three years along with many of his teammates. When he returned in 1946 he hit .335 and the team won 104 games. He was blamed by some who didn't know better for "holding the ball" in Game 7 of the '46 Series against St. Louis when Enos Slaughter made his "mad dash" from first base all the way around to score after a two-out bloop double to center field by Harry Walker. The play was in no way Pesky's fault. If anyone was to blame, it was center fielder Leon Culberson, who made a rainbow throw to Pesky in the cutoff position.

Pesky came back in '47 and hit .335, his highest average. The next year he hit .324. Over a 10-year career he hit .307 and had an on-base percentage of .394. He never struck out more than 36 times in a season (and that was in his rookie year). Never a power hitter, he hit only 17 homers in his career.

Said Pesky of his Pesky Pole namesake: "Mel Parnell started that. I won a game with a home run down the right-field line against the Athletics. Elmer Valo nearly broke his elbow trying to catch it. But I didn't have any power, and I knew it."

Pesky was traded to Detroit in 1952. After his playing career came to an end with the Washington Senators in 1954, Pesky, who roomed with Harmon Killebrew that season, became a coach and manager in the Yankees organization. He first served as a coach under Ralph Houk for the Denver Bears. He was a manager in the Tigers organization from 1956 to 1960 and took over the Red Sox's Triple A managing job in Seattle in 1961. By the end of the 1962 season Pesky was named manager of the Red Sox, but he had two poor seasons despite introducing Tony Conigliaro to the big leagues at age 19.

Pesky was fired late in the 1964 season. He went on to the Pittsburgh organization and, in a bizarre twist of fate, became first-base coach for Harry Walker—the very man who had stroked the double that enabled Slaughter to score from first in Game 7 of the '46 Series against St. Louis—from 1965 to 1967. After being somewhat miscast in radio and TV in Boston from 1969 to 1974, Pesky was hired to be a coach on Darrell Johnson's staff in 1975 and later became bench and hitting coach for Don Zimmer. When Zimmer was fired with five games to go in the 1980 season, Pesky served out those final five days. His last managing experience came in 1990, when he spent two and a half months as the manager of the Pawtucket Red Sox after Ed Nottle was fired in June of that season.

# 39 A Helluva Feller

"Attention please, ladies and gentlemen, boys and girls, welcome to Fenway Park."

That was public-address announcer Sherm Feller's unforgettable salutation to Red Sox fans at Fenway for 26 years. Feller was both informative and entertaining. He was a great storyteller, having so much to share after decades as a radio performer and the composer of more than 1,000 songs.

The 1950s were his heyday as a songwriter, composing popular tunes such as "Summertime, Summertime," "My Baby's Coming Home," and "Snow, Snow, Beautiful Snow." He was married to singer Judy Valentine, who performed many of his songs. The Boston Pops also performed his music, and he was friends with Nat King Cole, Frank Sinatra, Sammy Davis Jr., and Tony Bennett.

Feller announced the lineups with his deep, succinct voice and oftentimes added a little humor or color to the announcements. Carl Beane, the current PA man at Fenway, is a Feller protégé who has tried to carry on Feller's methods.

One of my fondest remembrances of Feller came on a night at Fenway when the electricity went out. It was May 13, 1991; Ellis Burks had a 2–2 count and was awaiting Chicago right-hander Jack McDowell's next pitch when the entire ballpark went black.

Burks recalled, "It was one of the weirdest things I ever experienced, but the one reason why people didn't panic or get upset was Sherm Feller just keeping everybody calm and relaxing them with sing-alongs and stuff like that. It was pretty funny. I wondered whether people even wanted the lights to go back on or whether they wanted to hear 'The Sherm Feller Show.'"

There was emergency lighting along the aisles, but for the most part Feller urged patrons (31,023 that night) to stay put. This was the first real power outage at the ballpark in about 10 years; the one in 1981 had occurred during the day. It turned out there was a problem on Commonwealth Avenue, but Feller cracked, "Boston Edison is working on it right now. If they send us the bill, we'll pay it." He led the crowd in "Take Me Out to the Ballgame" and managed to sprinkle in a little humor while also trying to make sure that fans stayed in their seats and remained calm. He performed for 59 minutes for a nearly packed house. The game itself wasn't as entertaining.

"Sherm was one of those guys that, I wouldn't say you took for granted, but as a player he was the one who introduced your name as you came up and it was a sound I guess that you grew accustomed to. People really associated him with the ballpark, just like they did John Kiley when he played the organ. You just expected to hear that voice. There was comfort in it, I guess," Burks recalled.

Feller was a favorite of so many visiting broadcasters, but the one who had the most fun with him was Baltimore Orioles broadcaster and former Red Sox announcer Jon Miller. Whenever he came to Fenway, Miller would go into the PA booth and perform for half an inning impersonating Feller. Unless you saw Miller doing it, you couldn't tell the difference, and oftentimes Miller would slip in and out without anyone noticing unless it was mentioned on TV.

One of Feller's great joys was going to Chinatown after games to partake of his favorite dish, and he often stayed there telling stories until the wee hours of the morning. Feller, born on July 29, 1918, passed away on January 27, 1994.

# 40 Theo, the GM Bambino

By the ripe old age of 30, Theo Epstein had won his first championship as the architect of the 2004 Red Sox. By age 33 he had won his second World Series title. Not bad for a kid who grew up in Brookline, about a mile from Fenway Park, whose lifelong dream was to work for the Red Sox.

Epstein came to the Sox after the new ownership group of John Henry and Tom Werner appointed Larry Lucchino as the team's president/CEO after the 2002 season. Lucchino had previously run the Padres, where he employed Epstein, bringing him aboard to replace interim general manager Mike Port. Epstein was actually Lucchino's third choice for the Red Sox job; he had previously tried unsuccessfully to hire both Oakland's Billy Beane and his top assistant, J.P. Ricciardi, who became the GM for the Toronto Blue Jays. At age 28, Epstein became the man in charge of the organization.

Epstein graduated from Yale University and also went to the University of San Diego's School of Law, where he earned his law degree while holding various jobs with the Padres. Epstein certainly bought into the sabermetrics method of Bill James (which involves the analysis of baseball through objective evidence, especially baseball statistics), but he also values scouting and has managed to combine the two into a successful run with the Sox.

After the '03 season Epstein was able to trade for and sign Curt Schilling to a contract extension over Thanksgiving dinner at Schilling's Scottsdale home and nearly pulled off quite a coup in acquiring Alex Rodriguez from Texas, a trade that would have sent Manny Ramirez to the Rangers. Epstein would then have dealt Nomar Garciaparra to the White Sox for Magglio Ordonez, but the whole deal fell through when the Sox insisted that A-Rod reduce his salary. While A-Rod was willing, the Players' Association ruled against it, afraid of setting a precedent.

Epstein's Sox had a big year in 2003, when they led the majors in virtually every major offensive category, but the Sox lost Game 7 of the ALCS to the Yankees when Grady Little left Pedro Martinez in too long. Epstein pulled off other major deals to build up the '04 team. He acquired Keith Foulke, who had played for the Oakland A's, as the team's closer. At the trading deadline on July 31 he swung a blockbuster of a three-team deal in which he traded shortstop Nomar Garciaparra and minor league outfielder Matt Murton to the Chicago Cubs and got back shortstop Orlando Cabrera from the Montreal Expos and slick-fielding first baseman Doug Mientkiewicz from the Minnesota Twins. He then acquired Dave Roberts from the Los Angeles Dodgers. All three players made a huge impact. Roberts's steal in Game 4 with the Sox on the verge of elimination allowed the Red Sox to come back from a 3–0 deficit against the Yankees in the ALCS to win four straight games. They then swept the St. Louis Cardinals in the World Series.

Epstein left the organization for a few months in October 2005 after turning down a three-year, $4.5 million deal. At the time he felt that the Sox hierarchy wasn't on the right page; he wanted more control over baseball operations and less interference from Lucchino. The Red Sox explored other options for a while, but it became clear that Epstein would return if certain conditions were met. On January 19, 2006, Epstein returned with complete control and began to rebuild the Sox for their '07 run after a disappointing '06 season in which injuries ruined the Sox's chances.

Epstein acquired J.D. Drew and Julio Lugo during the off-season and also bid $51.111 million for the right to negotiate with star Japanese right-hander Daisuke Matsuzaka. Epstein won a negotiating battle with superagent Scott Boras to sign Matsuzaka on the Sox's terms—six years and $52 million. Epstein also added Japanese lefty Hideki Okajima, who turned out to be one of the top set-up men in baseball. He introduced American League rookie of the year Dustin Pedroia to the everyday lineup at second base. The Red Sox spent 150 days in first place, swept the Angels in the American League Division Series, came back from a 3–1 deficit to beat the Indians in the American League Championship Series, and then swept the Colorado Rockies to win their second championship in four years—all under Epstein's guidance.

# 41 Trader Dick

Dick O'Connell became general manager on September 16, 1965, while the Red Sox were in the process of losing 100 games (it was also the same day that Dave Morehead threw a no-hitter at Fenway). From those very humble beginnings, O'Connell presided over two of the greatest teams in Red Sox history: the 1967 Impossible Dream Red Sox and the 1975 team that nearly upset the Cincinnati Reds' Big Red Machine.

It was O'Connell who made the decision to hire a young Dick Williams to manage; he then balked at having to fire him in 1969 but was overruled by owner Thomas Yawkey. He allowed the Sox farm system to crank out talent like Reggie Smith, Dwight Evans, Cecil Cooper, Ben Oglivie, Rick Burleson, Carlton Fisk, Fred Lynn, Jim Rice, Butch Hobson, and so many others, while at the same time acquiring key veterans like Gary Bell, Jerry Adair, Elston Howard, Norm Siebern, and Ken "Hawk" Harrelson during the 1967 season.

O'Connell's deals truly shaped the Red Sox of the late '60s and '70s. He dealt the popular Dick Radatz to Cleveland in June of '66 and got back Don McMahon and Lee Stange. That same year he acquired closer John Wyatt and outfielder Jose Tartabull—who helped dramatically in '67—in a six-player deal with Kansas City. He picked up Luis Tiant from the scrap heap in the early 1970s and signed Orlando Cepeda as the team's first designated hitter. He signed Ray Culp in 1973. He acquired Luis Aparicio to be his shortstop in 1971.

O'Connell pulled off a 10-player deal with Milwaukee on October 10, 1971, in which Jim Lonborg, Ken Brett, Billy

Conigliaro, Joe Lahoud, George Scott, and Don Pavletich were traded for Marty Pattin, Lew Krausse, Tommy Harper, and Pat Skrable. Harper is still the Red Sox's best all-time single-season base stealer with 54 steals. O'Connell flipped Pattin to Kansas City in October 1973 to acquire Dick Drago, who became Boston's closer in 1975.

During the 1973 off-season O'Connell also secured a big deal that helped the Sox in '75, trading Reggie Smith and Ken Tatum to St. Louis for Rick Wise and Bernie Carbo. On June 14, 1975, he acquired Denny Doyle from California in exchange for Chuck Ross. He also signed three familiar names: Tim McCarver, Gene Michael, and Juan Marichal. His big free-agent signing came in the winter of 1976, when he inked closer Bill Campbell.

O'Connell made tough decisions, including releasing Frank Malzone and Rico Petrocelli and trading Tony Conigliaro in 1970 (only to sign him back before the 1975 season). His worst deal? Probably sending lefty reliever Sparky Lyle to the Yankees in March 1972 for first baseman Danny Cater. Lyle had a great career for the Yanks.

O'Connell, a native of Winthrop, Massachusetts, and a 1937 graduate of Boston College, was indeed one of the most important figures in Red Sox history. In many ways he helped put baseball back on the map again. O'Connell's greatest contribution was moving away from the racism that seemed to have permeated the Red Sox organization for so long. Under his regime there were more African American players and many more Latin players added to the Boston roster.

O'Connell was fired by Mrs. Jean Yawkey in 1977 when the ownership reorganized after Thomas Yawkey's death in 1976 and Haywood Sullivan became a partner and the GM. O'Connell died on August 18, 2002, at age 87.

# 42 Lou, Lou, Lou

Lou Gorman brought many things to the Red Sox, but his biggest contribution might have been making the team a kinder and friendlier organization. Gorman was a personable baseball man basically brought in by Sox owner Haywood Sullivan to take the spotlight off him. Sullivan had been serving a dual role as co-owner and GM since Dick O'Connell was fired after the 1977 season. Sullivan never enjoyed answering questions for the media, but Gorman had a knack for it.

Gorman was a veteran baseball man, born and raised in Rhode Island, who had served in the navy and got his feet wet in the Baltimore Orioles organization. He was a key front-office member during the early success of the expansion Kansas City Royals team and then became general manager of the expansion Seattle Mariners, where he also built a successful organization. He next went to work for his longtime mentor Frank Cashen with the New York Mets and then landed his dream job with the Red Sox in 1984, the same year Roger Clemens debuted for the team.

Gorman brought a distinctive developmental philosophy to Boston. By 1986 he had not only brought along the Sox's young talent but had also made a few significant deals that put the Sox in the driver's seat. It didn't hurt when Clemens emerged as the would-be MVP and Cy Young winner in the American League. Ironically, Gorman had a huge hand in building the 1986 Mets, the team he would face and come one strike away from beating in the World Series.

Gorman started beefing up the Sox in the winter of 1985, obtaining Calvin Schiraldi and Wes Gardner from the Mets and swapping Mike Easler to the Yankees for Don Baylor, who became a clubhouse leader in 1986. Gorman acquired lefty reliever Joe Sambito off the scrap heap and shipped off shortstop Jackie Gutierrez to Baltimore for middle man Sammy Stewart.

He acquired top utility man Ed Romero from Milwaukee for reliever Mark Clear. Later in the year he sent Steve Lyons to the White Sox for an aging Tom Seaver in order to add a veteran presence to the starting rotation. Before you knew it, Gorman, who had already acquired Bill Buckner back in '84, had quite a team, with veterans Dwight Evans and Jim Rice also still in their prime. He also shipped off young shortstop Rey Quinones to the Mariners and got back Spike Owen and Dave Henderson, who really solidified the team.

The '86 team—except for a few veterans—had a homegrown flavor, particularly the starting rotation of Clemens, Al Nipper, Bruce Hurst, Dennis "Oil Can" Boyd, and a bullpen with Bob Stanley and Steve Crawford.

Gorman presided over playoff teams in 1988 and 1990 and developed a host of young talent, from Ellis Burks to Mo Vaughn. He's also the man who traded Jeff Bagwell to Houston in 1990 for Larry Andersen at a time when the Sox had depth at third base with Boggs, Steve Lyons, and Tim Naehring. He also acquired Mike Boddicker in 1988 for Curt Schilling and Brady Anderson.

Gorman was not afraid to wheel and deal. During his tenure he had to fire John McNamara and Joe Morgan and also made pitching relevant again in the Sox system. When Morgan took over as interim manager in 1988, Gorman had already secured Joe Torre as the new manager, but Morgan's success tied Gorman's hands, and he had no choice but to name Morgan as the permanent manager.

Gorman almost brought Kirby Puckett to Boston, making him a competitive offer, but Puckett elected to finish his career in Minnesota.

# 43 Tony C.

If you were a kid who loved the Red Sox in the 1960s, you likely had one hero: Tony Conigliaro. He was the local boy from Swampscott who had played baseball at St. Mary's of Lynn; he had so much charisma that an entire generation of baseball fans fell in love with him. He was the heartthrob of young girls in the Boston area. Conig was on his way to being a superstar and probably would have become one of the all-time home-run hitters. His wide stance, powerful frame, and sweet uppercut stroke made him perfectly suited to Fenway Park. The Green Monster looked like a tame little puppy to him.

Conigliaro stroked his first major league hit on April 16, 1964, at Yankee Stadium, a sixth-inning single against Whitey Ford, who went 11 innings that day in a loss. His first major league home run came against White Sox right-hander Joel Horlen on April 17 in the second game of the 1964 season. By 1967 it was all right there in front of him. Through mid-August he had already hit 20 homers and driven in 67 runs. On July 23 at Cleveland, Conigliaro became the youngest player, at just 22 years old, to reach 100 homers, when he stroked a John O'Donoghue fastball into the left-field seats with Joe Foy aboard in the first inning. Yes, sir, No. 25 was something special.

But on August 18, smack in the middle of the Impossible Dream season, our hero crumbled to the Fenway earth. In the bottom of the fourth inning he took a fastball from Angels righty Jack Hamilton square in the left eye. His athletic and normally limber body seemed frozen as the pitch overwhelmed him. He went down as if he'd been shot.

Conigliaro was always one to crowd the plate, something pitchers didn't care for. He had missed a month of his rookie season when Moe Drabowsky drilled him on his left wrist (Tony was only 19 years old at the time), and in a similar incident in 1965 Wes Stock broke Conig's left hand with a pitch. Hamilton has always denied that he threw at Conigliaro. After the beaning Conigliaro was rushed to Sancta Maria Hospital in Cambridge. He was out of baseball for all of 1968 while he struggled to recoup some of the vision in his left eye.

Tony C. made a comeback in 1969—and what a comeback it was. Conigliaro had found a way to see the baseball without really seeing it. On Opening Day in Baltimore's Memorial Stadium in '69, he batted fifth and played right field. He homered in the tenth inning off Pete Richert to give the Sox a 4–2 lead. He went 2-for-4 with two walks, a sign that he was indeed back. Tony C. hit .255 with 20 homers and 82 RBIs in '69. He came back in 1970 to have his best offensive season yet: 36 homers, 116 RBIs.

The Red Sox broke his heart when they traded him after the '70 season to California. But his eyesight was taking a turn for the worse. He played in only 74 games before it became clear that he wouldn't be able to play, and he was out of the game from 1972 to 1974. He again had a comeback in 1975, although this one was brief. On Opening Day at Fenway, Conig batted cleanup and served as designated hitter. The Red Sox were playing the Brewers, whose DH that day was Hank Aaron. Conigliaro, now 30 years old, who had unsuccessfully tried to make it back as a pitcher during the three years he was out of the game, received a long, warm ovation that day. This reporter, a college student at Northeastern University at the time, was one of the people standing up to applaud. Tony C. singled in his first at-bat, but he would not be able to sustain it. He played his final game on June 12 at Comiskey Park. He went 0-for-3 to dip to .123 on the season, grounding out to second baseman Jorge Orta in the eighth inning. That was the last of Tony C.

Coningliaro became a sportscaster in San Francisco. In 1982, on his way to rehearsal for a Boston TV job, he suffered a heart attack and a stroke. He spent the last eight years of his life as an invalid and died at the age of 45.

# 44 The Dice-K Invasion

The highly touted Barry Zito was out there for the taking in the free-agent market in the winter of 2006, but the Red Sox only had eyes for Daisuke Matsuzaka, a 26-year-old phenom from the Seibu Lions of the Japanese Pacific League who had won the World Baseball Classic's MVP award.

A group of international Red Sox scouts, including Craig Shipley, Jon Deeble, assistant general manager Jed Hoyer, general manager Theo Epstein, and president Larry Lucchino, skillfully put together a sealed bid of $51.111 million—which, as it turned out, blew away the New York Mets ($39 million), the Texas Rangers ($34 million), and the New York Yankees ($30 million)—landing the coveted pitcher with one proviso: negotiating a deal with super-agent Scott Boras.

"There were certainly a lot of ups and downs as far as the nego-tiations," said Epstein of the historic deal. "But I think all the parties had a common goal: just for Daisuke to join the Red Sox and start his major league career."

The Red Sox brass had taken a proactive approach with the negotiations, which eventually yielded a six-year, $52 million deal. Boras had very little leverage in the negotiations other than the threat of having his client return to pitch in Japan. He had been talking about Matsuzaka in the same way as his other free-agent clients, including Zito, who signed a seven-year, $126 million deal with the San Francisco Giants. But in the end, what rang true was

*Daisuke Matsuzaka, more commonly known as "Dice-K," has become a Red Sox star since his acquisition at the end of 2006.*

that as far as a contract was concerned, Matsuzaka was really no different from any other rookie coming to the majors—the Red Sox had six years of control over him before he could become a free agent. Boras tried to negotiate to allow Matsuzaka to become a free agent sooner by placing a provision in the deal, but the Red Sox held their ground.

The key turn of events might have come when Sox owner John Henry flew his negotiators, Lucchino and Epstein, to Southern California on his private jet in an attempt to reach an 11th-hour deal. Another key moment came when Boras and Matsuzaka got on a plane back to Boston; Boras negotiated the deal with the Sox brass during the flight while Matsuzaka slept. The Red Sox won the salary negotiations but also agreed to many perks, including providing the pitcher with massage and physical therapists, a personal assistant, an interpreter, and close to 100 flights to allow his wife and daughter to travel back and forth from Japan. The December 14, 2006, press conference to announce the deal was considered the most attended media conference in the city's history; more than 300 international media people attended.

Dice-K, as he is nicknamed, had his ups and downs in his rookie season in the majors. He was strong early but struggled late, a sign that adapting to major league life was difficult after seven seasons in Japan. The Red Sox did everything they could to ease the culture shock, employing translators to help him handle the media and protecting him from outside influences. They provided him with the best places to live, eat, and shop, away from "the maddening crowd," and did all they could not to overload him with media requests. Dice-K and pitching coach John Farrell learned to communicate beyond gestures and signs; each learned words in the other's language to compliment the universal language of baseball.

Early in the season Dice-K's starts were major events. They surpassed anything the Red Sox had experienced with Pedro Martinez and Roger Clemens during their long and illustrious tenures with the Red Sox. Japanese culture infiltrated Boston more than ever, with Japanese restaurants sprouting up everywhere in the city.

There were flashbulbs and a great deal of hype on those nights when Dice-K matched up against Seattle center fielder Ichiro Suzuki or New York's Hideki Matsui, both fellow crossovers from Japan. Dice-K and Ichiro had developed a friendship back home, and the two had lunch right before spring training. It was Ichiro's way of trying to help his friend learn about what to expect and ease into his first season of major league baseball.

Swarms of Japanese media covered every one of Dice-K's starts, both at Fenway and on the road, and his games were broadcast live in Japan, often at 2:00 or 3:00 AM. The Red Sox were so concerned about the sheer volume of Japanese media that they remodeled the Fenway press box to add more seating and enlarged the media room so spillover Japanese media could watch games on big-screen TVs and then have access to postgame press conferences, which Dice-K engaged in for both the Japanese and American media. He also agreed to interviews with the Japanese media between starts to update them on the news of the week. From his trouble with the major league mounds, to cutbacks and changes to his workouts, to ongoing stories about the difference in baseballs between the two countries, Dice-K was always making news back in Japan.

The Major League ball felt far more slippery than what Dice-K was used to in Japan, which hindered his ability to throw his vast repertoire of pitches (something that had been exaggerated slightly from the moment he was signed). Some Daisuke experts said he threw up to six different pitches, but that myth died fast. In fact, by September Dice-K was throwing too many fastballs and not enough of his off-speed stuff.

Matsuzaka's pitch counts were monitored closely throughout the season. In Japan it is not unheard of to throw 160 or 170 pitches in a game, which Dice-K had done on a few occasions. In Boston he was allowed to throw one game of 130 pitches and three of 120 or more, but in June, Boras expressed concern that his client might be throwing too many pitches and thought it best for the Red Sox to limit him to something closer to 100 pitches per game.

Matsuzaka had been billed as a workhorse with a rubber arm. That was evident by his early-season workout regimen, for which he threw considerably more than major league pitchers do between starts, even playing long toss before he pitched. But it was also evident that he was human, and the season took its toll. Dice-K went through one particularly horrid stretch in September during which he went 1–4 with a 9.58 ERA. At that point there were questions as to whether he was suffering from fatigue from the grind of the major league season (the Japanese season is only 140 games long). Sox manager Terry Francona, who was never willing to acknowledge that fatigue might have been a factor, did concede that the intensity of the season, the extra travel (which Dice-K was not used to), and the grind of it all did come into play. Matsuzaka seemed to get his second wind in a five-and-two-thirds-innings stint against the New York Yankees on September 14 in which he walked five and hit a batter, allowing two runs and throwing 120 pitches.

The Red Sox were determined to have him as one of their top three starters in the playoffs, and Dice-K came up big in the postseason, winning Game 7 of the ALCS and Game 3 of the World Series. Looks like big things ahead...

# 45 Morgan's Magic

To understand "Morgan's Magic," you have to understand just how dark things felt around Fenway in 1988. Still recovering from the kick in the teeth of the 1986 World Series, the 1987 Red Sox came out as flat as they had ended the previous season. A 9–13 April led to a woeful 78–84 season despite stellar years from Wade Boggs, who won a batting title with a .363 average; Roger Clemens, who won his second straight Cy Young with a 20–9 record and a 2.63 ERA after starting with losses in his first two starts; and Dwight Evans, who had a .305 average with 34 homers and 123 RBIs.

In early 1988 the situation hadn't improved. The Red Sox were up and down. In June the team was rocked by the Wade Boggs–Margo Adams scandal, in which a Costa Mesa, California, woman filed a $6 million palimony suit against Boggs. There were team skirmishes stemming from the Boggs incident when the team caught wind that depositions would be taken in the case, something which could cause a few players some personal embarrassment.

It didn't help matters when Rich Gedman hit the foul pole down the right-field line in Kansas City in early June and umpire Dale Scott called it foul! The Sox lost the game 8–7.

But the real problem was that John McNamara had seemingly lost control of the team. The Sox stumbled their way through Kansas City, Minnesota, and Chicago, losing eight out of 12. After a 4–1 loss to the White Sox just before the All-Star break, McNamara uttered his final words as manager: "After all is said and done and all we've been through, I'm very happy to be one game over .500." Ownership was not so happy. As the season was about to resume after the break, the Sox called a press conference at Fenway announcing that McNamara had been fired. Joe Morgan was hired as the "interim manager."

And suddenly there was a breath of fresh air around Fenway.

Walpole Joe Morgan was a local guy who had worked plowing snow on the Massachusetts Turnpike during the Blizzard of '78. He was a coach on McNamara's staff, but you'd never find two men so different from one another.

"My job is to get faith into this ballclub," Morgan said. Winning 12 straight and 19 out of 20 will do that.

Morgan made one big positional change: Jody Reed became his shortstop and Spike Owen was benched. His first game as manager was rained out, but the Sox won a doubleheader against the Royals the next day. Morgan won the next 10 before losing to the Texas Rangers 9–8 despite a Sox rally to score three in the seventh. The tying run, Ellis Burks, was stranded on second base with two outs in the ninth when Todd Benzinger, who had been a force during this run, lined out hard to left to end the game.

But the Sox then rattled off seven more wins. A big player during this stretch was Kevin Romine, who stroked his first homer—a game winner—in a 7–6 Sox win over Kansas City after Boston came from behind, 6–0. Morgan clashed with superstar Jim Rice along the way, once bringing up Owen to pinch hit for Rice because the situation called for a bunt.

Sox general manager Lou Gorman had lined up Joe Torre to be the next manager of the Red Sox, but after Morgan's unexpected success, he had no choice but to name Morgan the permanent manager, which he did on July 20. Gorman then put together a huge deal to reinforce the pitching staff, trading young players Curt Schilling and Brady Anderson to Baltimore for veteran righty Mike Boddicker. Boddicker's first start, on July 31, was a 5–0 shutout win over Milwaukee in which he hurled seven and a third scoreless innings.

The Sox went into first place for good on September 5, cementing the reputation of "Morgan's Magic." They beat the Yankees five out of seven in September; the acquisition of Boddicker paid off, as he picked up the slack of a slumping Roger Clemens. The Sox won the American League East with 89 wins, but they definitely lost some of their sizzle at the end of the season, losing 10 out of their last 11 games, including being swept in four games by the Oakland A's in the American League Championship Series. Even in the playoffs, Morgan did things his own way. He pinch hit for both Rice and Evans in Game 4, ruffling feathers.

It is clear that in the end, the Sox were simply outplayed. "These guys are good," said Morgan of the A's, led by Jose Canseco's three homers and lights-out relief from Dennis Eckersley. "There is no question that they had a better club than we did, and it showed in the end. They had a little too much for us overall. I honestly thought the series would go better than this. But it's still the end of the line this year."

# 46 The Real Monster: Dick Radatz

Back at Fenway in the early '60s, the word *imposing* was spelled R-A-D-A-T-Z. During those lean years there was nothing to watch. Oh, there was a young Carl Yastrzemski, and in '64 along came Tony Conigliaro, but the reason fans turned on the game was to watch 6'5" closer Dick Radatz.

In those days closers were used a tad differently from how it's done today. In his first four season, Radatz pitched 124⅔, 132⅓, 157, and 124⅓ innings respectively. That would be equal to the number of innings some young starters in the big leagues pitch today. Radatz was not only imposing, he was nasty. There was no guessing what he would do. He'd throw a fastball, probably in the 95–100 mph range, and more often than not, the batter wouldn't be able to hit it.

Radatz had four incredible seasons from 1962 to '66, and then for some reason—whether he ran out of gas or hurt his arm—he was never the same. The sad part was that this jovial, fun-loving guy never got to experience the joy of the 1967 season; he was traded to Cleveland midway through the 1966 campaign, when it became obvious to GM Dick O'Connell that he had lost something off his fastball.

Radatz had actually developed a sore arm in the minors at Boston's Seattle Triple A affiliate in 1961. He begged his manager, Johnny Pesky, to let him continue as a starter, but that wasn't in the cards. Anyway, Radatz's real calling was obvious. He came into a game when it needed to be held. Sometimes that was as early as the fifth inning. Radatz pitched some unbelievable stretches.

On June 9 and 11, 1963, he pitched six innings against Detroit, got a day off, and then pitched eight and two-thirds innings against the Orioles. In 1965 he faced the Yankees on September 4 and went three and two thirds innings, then came back the next day and pitched six innings. He often closed both games of a doubleheader.

Radatz was known for his sheer and utter domination of Yankees great Mickey Mantle, whom he faced 19 times in his career and struck out 12 times. There was no pitcher Mantle feared more than Radatz. It was Mantle who nicknamed him "the Monster." After one tough game Mantle was heard to snap "that monster!"—and so the nickname was born. Mantle often told teammates, "I knew exactly what he was going to throw and where he was going to throw it, and I still couldn't hit it."

Radatz was extremely demonstrative on the mound; whenever he struck out a batter, he clenched his fist in the air and pumped it, a show of emotion that many modern-day closers have adopted. It's a shame that Radatz's dominance was wasted on such poor teams. He went 15–6 with 25 saves in 1963 and 16–9 with 29 saves in 1964.

Radatz, who grew up outside of Detroit and played baseball and basketball at Michigan State, stayed in the Boston area after his career ended following the 1969 season. He went into private business while also appearing on sports talk radio and TV in Boston. He also coached the North Shore Spirit of the Independent League.

Radatz was old school and could never understand the way modern closers were used. "If I could have pitched one inning at a time, I would have pitched for 20 years," he often told me. "Back when I pitched, I knew I wasn't starting and I knew I'd be used to finish off a game. But sometimes that was seven or eight innings. Didn't bother me a bit. I wanted the ball the next day. I'd pitch anytime, any place. But it's all timing I guess. The game and the role changed so much over the years that I probably could have been a dominant closer making millions of dollars. For that kind of money I'd even pitch two innings a time."

Radatz suffered from severe circulation problems later in life. He died at 67 years old when he lost his balance in his home and fell down the stairs.

# 47 The Third Base Saloon

Nuf Ced McGreevy was the all-time greatest Red Sox fan. He owned the Third Base Saloon, where Boston Americans/Red Sox and Boston Braves fans gathered to discuss the baseball issues of the day. Located at 940 Columbus Avenue in Boston, it was so named because "It's the last place you go before home." It was the place to go to exchange Red Sox information and talk before the existence of sports radio and websites.

There were often huge arguments among the patrons, but the final judge and jury was McGreevy himself, who was nicknamed Nuf Ced because he would slam his fist on the bar before having what he considered the final word on any given subject. His bar featured newspaper articles, old sports photographs, and all kinds of baseball memorabilia that were eventually donated to the Boston Public Library.

McGreevy was the leader of the Royal Rooters, an influential fan group that the team's ownership couldn't ignore. They would often meet at the Third Base Saloon to state their strong opinions on everything team management did in terms of personnel, and no team executive—or manager, for that matter—wanted to get on their bad side. They had a brass band, and they constantly played their theme song, "Tessie" (which came from the Broadway musical *The Silver Slipper*), at every home game.

The Rooters attended the first World Series between the Boston Americans and the Pittsburgh Pirates in 1903, making a real nuisance of themselves (which was precisely their goal). The media even blamed them in part for the Americans losing one of the games at Huntington Avenue Grounds because the standing-room-only crowd was within a few feet of the actual playing field. The Rooters followed the Series to Pittsburgh and jeered at the Pirates, playing verses of "Tessie" over and over again to annoy them.

The Royal Rooters were really put off on October 15, 1912, when they entered Fenway at 1:40 PM for Game 7 of the World Series and found that their customary seats, in the bleachers past the third-base line, were already occupied by an overflow crowd. The Rooters caused quite a ruckus as they spilled over onto the field, where they had a rhubarb with the mounted police, delaying the start of the game some 25 minutes.

During Prohibition the Third Base Saloon had to shut down, and that pretty much put an end to the Royal Rooters. But in their day, they were the original fan club.

The Rooters gave way to the BoSox Club, which was founded in 1967 at the height of the Impossible Dream season. The club has grown enormously over the years. They call themselves "an organization of the fans, by the fans, and for the fans. It is the voice of the fans in all matters regarding the Boston Red Sox and their affiliate organizations. The Club is recognized by the Boston Red Sox as the oldest, the largest, and the official fan organization supporting Boston baseball." The BoSox Club also does a great deal of charitable work on behalf of Red Sox charities.

Another powerful Sox fans group is the Sons of Sam Horn (SOSH), which has a strong following on the Internet through their website.

# 48 Four!

Red Sox fans don't really like to think about those Yankees types. But there's one Yankee we should remember and actually thank: Chase Wright. He's the kid who served four consecutive home runs to the Red Sox on April 22, 2007. It was only the fifth time four consecutive homers had occurred in baseball history. All of this happened with two outs on the board, by the way.

There has been only one other time in baseball history when one hurler threw four dingers in a row, and the name of that fellow probably won't roll off your tongue—it was Paul Foytack in a game that took place on July 31, 1963.

"I just tried to stay calm and cool," Wright told reporters after a game that concluded a three-game sweep by the Red Sox at Fenway Park. "You don't feel like that's acceptable."

I wouldn't think so either.

"I've never seen that happen," said Mike Lowell. "Not even in Little League."

Very few people have. The 1961 Braves did it with Eddie Mathews, Hank Aaron, Joe Adcock, and Frank Thomas. The 1963 Indians did it with Woodie Held, Pedro Ramos, Tito Francona (father of manager Terry Francona), and Larry Brown. The 1964

Twins did it with Tony Oliva, Bobby Allison, Jimmie Hall, and Harmon Killebrew. And the 2006 Dodgers performed the feat with Jeff Kent, J.D. Drew, Russell Martin, and Marlon Anderson. And yes—for those of you playing at home—this means that for two years in a row, J.D. Drew was a player on a team that pulled off this rare feat. Quite an odd coincidence!

"It was amazing the first time I did it with the Dodgers," said Drew. "To have been part of it two straight years.... You would never believe that possible. But it's one of those contagious things. When you come up and the guy in front of you has hit one, you're looking for the same kind of pitch to hit and drive and when it comes and it happens, it's like wow!"

The other oddity is that it took Wright only 10 pitches to deliver the four throws that turned into homers for Manny Ramirez, Drew, Lowell, and Jason Varitek in the third inning. Those four blows reversed a 3–0 Yankees lead, giving Boston a 4–3 margin; they fell behind again, 5–4, before Lowell hit a three-run homer to bury the Yankees for good.

# 49 The First World Series

Yes, given that Boston has won only seven World Series, it's hard to believe sometimes that they played in the very first one.

Their habit of coming back from a big hole started way back then. The Americans had to fight back from a 3–1 deficit to beat the Pittsburgh Pirates five games to three in what at the time was a best-of-nine Series. This was the first World Series of the 20th century; although several so-called Series had been played in the late 1800s, those games were considered to be only exhibitions.

*A view of the Huntington Avenue Grounds during the 1903 World Series—the first World Series in history—between the Pittsburgh Pirates and the Boston Red Sox (then called the Boston Americans).*

Winning in 1903 was no small feat; the Pirates were the hottest team of that era. They had won three consecutive National League pennants. The National League was, at the time, the dominant league—the senior circuit. But in 1903 the Pirates' performance was hurt by a handful of injuries.

Still called the Americans at that point, the future Red Sox had the edge on the mound, and even then pitching was the name of the game. They got three wins from Bill Dinneen and two from Cy Young. The Americans were also helped immensely by the moral support they received from their Royal Rooters, who made the trek to Pittsburgh for the away games.

The Americans apparently felt at home in Pittsburgh, defeating the Pirates three straight to take a 4–3 lead in the Series. Pirates fans, trying to outdo the Rooters, actually threw confetti on the pitcher's mound before Dinneen started in Game 6, but the prank had the opposite affect—Dineen got mad, and then he got even. The Rooters teased Pirates star Honus Wagner by singing the song "Tessie" with specially rewritten lyrics that went something like "Honus, why do you hit so badly." The joke seemed to agitate the Pirates star.

The Series then went back to Boston, where Dinneen pitched a four-hit shutout at Huntington Avenue Grounds despite opening up a cut on one of the fingers on his pitching hand during the third inning. He pitched the rest of the game, with trickles of blood often leaking out, to clinch the Series.

# 50 Where Have You Gone, Dom DiMaggio?

When we spoke not long ago, the thing Dom DiMaggio seemed most proud of in his major league career is that he made it to the majors wearing glasses. DiMaggio, known as "the Little Professor" because his glasses made him look studious, was always told he'd never make it to the big leagues because his eyesight just wasn't up to it, and glasses would impede his ability to play at a high level. Maybe the critics were right, in that he never reached the heights of his brother Joe. But Dom played at a near-Hall-of-Fame level during 10 seasons as the Red Sox's center fielder.

It's amazing to think that he patrolled center in Boston at the same time Joe did so in New York. During Joe's 56-game hitting streak in 1941, Dom would get updates from Ted Williams while on the field; Williams got them from the guy who worked inside the Wall in left at Fenway.

Dominic never complained about how much more adulation his brother received, or about the fact that he always played second fiddle. He was just grateful that he got to play in the majors, that he played well, and that he got to share his experience with Joe.

Dom and Joe were certainly different on and off the field. Joe was a handsome, strapping, 6'1" man-about-town who dated starlets before and after his marriage to Marilyn Monroe. Dominic was a bespectacled, 5'9" contact hitter who fell in love with a girl named Emily, to whom he was married for more than 60 years. Joe was a recluse after his playing days, while Dom was very open and friendly, becoming a successful businessman after retiring from the game.

Dom had his own unbroken hitting streak—34 games in 1949, which remains a Red Sox record. "I can't believe that's still a record," DiMaggio said. "When you're going through it, you never imagine that it will hold up for that long. The Red Sox have had so many great hitters since that. You would think that someone would have broken it by now. But I'm reminded of it a lot."

DiMaggio was a .298 career hitter who was named to seven All-Star Games. He hit .316 in 1946 with seven homers and 73 RBIs; in 1950 he hit .328 with seven homers and 70 RBIs. He had an on-base percentage that season of .414, and he led the league with 11 triples.

He was also a great center fielder who could really track down the ball. Johnny Pesky, his beloved teammate, said of DiMaggio's skills, "He was the perfect player. He never made a mistake. He was the kind of guy who would go through a wall to win a ballgame. He was just such a perfect piece for the type of team we had."

# 51 On a Roll

The Sox were a great team in 1912, winning a team-record 105 games behind the great Tris Speaker, who won the American League MVP award with a .383 average, 10 homers, and 90 RBIs while playing a great center field. Yet Boston had started the Series as underdogs, facing a Giants team that featured Hall of Fame pitchers Christy Mathewson and Rube Marquard.

Boston had Smoky Joe Wood, who was 34–5 during the regular season, and perhaps the best-fielding outfield ever in Duffy Lewis, Speaker, and Harry Hooper. In a World Series that rivaled 1975's classic as the most dramatic championship ever, Wood beat the Giants three times, winning Game 8 (Game 2 was halted because of darkness with the score tied) in relief. The Sox scored two off Mathewson in the bottom of the tenth after center fielder Red Snodgrass muffed an easy fly and the Giants allowed a foul pop-up to drop. Snodgrass, like teammate Fred Merkle—whose baserunning gaffe cost the Giants the 1908 pennant—was constantly reminded of his "$30,000 Muff" (coming in second cost the Giants players $30,000 in championship pay).

The Red Sox wound up rallying to win the game 3–2 against the great Mathewson in what is considered the greatest World Series of the dead-ball era. Wood, who had a sore arm, came on to relieve starting pitcher Hugh Bedient. The Giants took a 2–1 lead in the tenth, but in the bottom of the inning Clyde Engle took second base on the Snodgrass error. Steve Yerkes walked. Engle scored on a Speaker single when the Giants gave Speaker a second chance after failing to catch a pop foul. The Red Sox eventually won on a Larry Gardner sacrifice fly that scored Yerkes with the winning run.

The 1915 Sox were another absolutely dominant team, winning 101 games and defeating the Philadelphia Phillies in the World Series in five games. The public was so enthusiastic about the Sox that the team couldn't even play at Fenway and were forced to use the larger Braves Field. Can you imagine a team that was so dominant that it didn't have to use Babe Ruth *or* Smoky Joe Wood on their World Series pitching staff? All they needed was Dutch Leonard, Ernie Shore, and Rube Foster to beat up the Phillies, holding their lineup to a .182 average. The Sox pitchers outdueled a Phillies staff led by Grover Cleveland Alexander, who actually beat the Sox in Game 1, 3–1. Right fielder Harry Hooper smacked two home runs, including the winner in a 5–4 Game 7 win. Power, pitching, and great defense—it all added up to a world championship.

In 1916 Bill Carrigan did a great managing job; although Speaker had been traded before the start of the season over a contract dispute and Wood held out all season over a contract issue as well, Ruth won 23 games with a 1.75 ERA. Ruth pitched brilliantly in a 2–1 win in 14 innings in Game 2 of the Series when Del Gainer knocked in Mike McNally for the winning run. The Sox roughed up Brooklyn's Marquard twice in the Series. Shore won two big Series games, including the fifth and final game, at Braves Field on October 12 as the Red Sox captured back-to-back World Series championships.

# 52 Two Games in '49

Long before the playoff game between the Yankees and the Red Sox in 1978, the two teams squared off for the pennant in 1949. This was another missed opportunity in a line of many for the Olde Town Team. They held a one-game lead with two to play. If they held on, they would win the pennant and go on to the World Series. If they lost, the season was over.

Well, I think everyone knows what happened next: the Sox dropped the weekend series to the Yanks at Yankee Stadium.

The Yankees won the Saturday game 5–4 when Johnny Lindell belted the go-ahead eighth-inning homer. Then Yankees lefty Joe Page held the Sox at bay over the final five and two-thirds innings. Heading into Sunday the Sox were starting 23-game winner Ellis Kinder while the Yankees gave the nod to Vic Raschi. Both teams had all of their starters available to pitch if need be. The Sox had 25-game winner Mel Parnell in reserve.

The odds seemed pretty good that they might win a game, huh? Unfortunately, as *The New York Times'* Dave Anderson wrote, Kinder was out drinking with old friend and *Daily Mirror* sportswriter Arthur Richman until 4:00 AM on Saturday night. Richman confirmed this to Anderson, but no problem. Kinder, 35 at the time, had a 7–2 career mark against the Yanks, 4–0 during the '49 season. He slept it off and pitched pretty well, trailing the Yanks 1–0 into the seventh inning.

It was here that manager Joe McCarthy intervened when he shouldn't have. He pinch hit for Kinder in the eighth and brought on Parnell in the bottom of the inning. Sound thinking? Perhaps it seemed that way at the time, but Parnell was shelled for four runs, three of which came when Sox right fielder Al Zarilla attempted and missed a shoestring catch of a Jerry Coleman double. Though the Sox scored three in the ninth, it wasn't enough; the Yankees won, 5–3. That was the first of five consecutive pennants and five consecutive World Series titles for the Yankees.

According to newspaper reports, Kinder had it out with McCarthy on the train ride home for making the decision to pinch hit for him. Sox owner Tom Yawkey told Kinder, "Two teams can't win the same pennant."

And the Red Sox wouldn't win any pennant until 1967.

# 53 1918

If it weren't for 2004 and 2007, the 1918 season would have been farther up in the order of importance in this book. But Red Sox fans everywhere can now finally say, "We don't care about 1918!" For 86 years they had been hearing about 1918, the last time they'd won a World Series. Who wasn't tired of hearing "1918"? It was the subject of every dig and bad joke. Finally, fans can put it in its proper place in Sox history.

Oh, sure, it was a significant season for many reasons. The Sox won it all in six games over the Cubs. This was during World War I, when more than 100 players from around the country went off to battle. The Sox had only four players left from the 1916 championship team: Carl Mays and Babe Ruth as pitchers along with right fielder Harry Hooper and shortstop Everett Scott as positional players.

Ruth became a dominant force as a pitcher that year. He went 13–7 with a 2.22 ERA in 19 starts and 20 games, blasted 11 homers and 66 RBIs, and hit .300. Doesn't sound like much? Consider that the rest of the league hit only 85 homers that season. In that context, Ruth was an exciting player.

Because it was wartime, the season was cut short, done by Labor Day. The Sox won the American League by two and a half games over Cleveland with a 75–51 record. They had excellent pitching, led by Mays, who went 21–13 and won two games in the World Series.

Ruth also won twice in the World Series and extended his scoreless innings streak to 29⅔ innings before the Cubs scored twice off him in Game 4 of a 3–2 Sox win. The big slugger had grown tired of pitching by then and wanted to become a full-time outfielder, but it wasn't meant to be in '18. At one point his relationship with manager Ed Barrow became so difficult that he quit the team for a few days to join the Chester Shipyards team in Pennsylvania after he'd been fined for missing a take sign. That was early July. Owner Harry Frazee threatened the team with legal action if they signed him, and Ruth came back a few days later to finish out the season.

Frazee, who would sell Ruth to the Yankees a year later, was actually a big-spending owner, aquiring four major players from the cash-strapped Athletics: center fielder Amos Strunk, first baseman Stuffy McInnis, catcher Wally Schang, and pitcher Joe Bush. The new additions proved to be the major reason why the Sox were better than the rest of the pack.

Ruth had a 1.06 ERA in his two World Series wins. He hit only .200 but had only five at-bats. As much as Ruth wanted to be more of a force offensively, Barrow went with George Whiteman in the outfield in the Series. This proved to be an excellent move, as Whiteman made several tremendous catches in left field, none greater than the one he made on a somersaulting grab in Game 6 to rob the Cubs' Turner Barber of a hit in the eighth, preserving a one-run (2–1) lead for Mays.

The Series was also unique because the players staged a brief strike before Game 5, disgruntled over the way game receipts were being split for the players. The fans were pretty angry over the dispute. Player rep Harry Hooper and Cubs player rep Les Mann negotiated with Major League Baseball to no avail, but the players finally agreed to take the field in tribute to the wounded soldiers and for the good of the country. The strike didn't go over well with Boston fans, who decided to stay away for the deciding Game 6. Only 15,238 spectators were on hand to watch Mays's excellent pitching effort and Whiteman's defensive heroics.

# 54 Mad Dash

Teddy Ballgame had a .342 average with 38 homers and 123 RBIs upon his return to baseball in 1946 after three years of military service. The '46 Sox were an offensive machine, scoring 792 runs in 154 games en route to 104 wins, the last team in Sox history to reach the century mark. They won the American League title by 12 games, ending a 28-year drought, and simply brought a good feeling to Boston again. They had an All-Star lineup including Williams, Bobby Doerr, Dom DiMaggio, Johnny Pesky, and Rudy York. York drove in 119 runs and Doerr knocked in 116, while Pesky hit .335 and DiMaggio .316 with 73 RBIs.

The Sox had pitching, too. Dave "Boo" Ferriss went 25–6 with a 3.25 ERA; Tex Hughson was 20–11 with a 2.75 ERA; lefty Mickey Harris went 17–9 with a 3.64 ERA; and Joe Dobson was 13–7 with a 3.24 ERA.

The Sox jumped out to a 21–3 start, winning 15 straight games, and then started a 12-game streak that took them to 41–9. They never really looked back after that. They came within a win of eclipsing the franchise record for wins—105 by the 1912 Sox—before finishing the last stretch of the season with a more pedestrian 13–10, clinching the pennant on September 13. The clincher was a 1–0 win behind a fantastic effort by Hughson and the only inside-the-park homer of Williams's career. Joe Cronin's team was the odds-on favorite to win the World Series over St. Louis, but they instead lost the championship that became famous for Enos Slaughter's "Mad Dash" in seven games.

The Sox might have been a tad worn out. They hadn't finished well and, instead of enjoying a respite while the National League tried to sort out its pennant winner in a playoff, they also scheduled three exhibition games at Fenway against what was essentially an All-Star squad of the top players around baseball. They feared getting rusty, but they likely wound up playing tired as a result. Adding to this poor decision was the fact that Williams was hit with a pitch in the right elbow during one of those exhibition games; his .200 average in the Series was blamed on the injury.

The Sox took Game 1 against St. Louis, 3–2, on York's tenth-inning homer at Sportsman's Park; reliever Earl Johnson shut the door on the Cards in the bottom of the inning. The Cards had to alter their rotation because of a two-game playoff against the Cincinnati Reds to decide the National League pennant, but in Game 2 of the World Series, Harry "the Cat" Brecheen spun a beauty against the Sox in a four-hitter, 3–0, while also driving in the winning run. When the Series returned to Boston, Ferriss threw a six-hit shutout. Williams beat the shift by dropping a bunt toward third for a base hit.

The good times didn't last in Game 4 as the Cardinals tied it two-all when they blasted Hughson—who was pitching on three days' rest—12–3. Williams was suffering from his elbow injury and the Sox also lost Doerr, who was suffering from a migraine headache, for Game 5. But Dobson picked the Sox up; with his 6–3 win they went up 3–2 in the Series. Dobson, who was Boston's fourth starter, allowed only four hits.

The Series then shifted back to St. Louis, where it sure seemed as though Boston would prove the experts right. Why do Sox managers make such poor decisions in the postseason? Hey, Grady Little couldn't be blamed for this one. Cronin did it all by himself. Instead of using Hughson or Ferriss to finish the Cardinals off, he decided to go to Harris, who had a good year but was a journeyman pitcher at best. As it turned out, the Sox offense was silenced by Brecheen. Doerr made a questionable decision to go from first to third on Higgins's single to left in the second inning and was thrown out, taking the Sox out of a potentially big inning. The Sox bowed 4–1.

Boston went out to a 1–0 lead in Game 7, but the Cardinals roared back against Ferriss to take a 3–1 lead. The Sox rallied back in the eighth to tie it off Brecheen, who had come on to relieve Murry Dickson in a bold move by Cards manager Eddie Dyer. DiMaggio stroked a two-run double but pulled his hamstring and had to leave the game. With the go-ahead run at second base, Williams popped out to end the rally.

Cronin again defied logic with a questionable managerial decision. The Cardinals had two left-handed hitters coming up. The situation was tailor-made for lefty Johnson, who had saved Game 1—right? But Cronin decided on righty Bob Klinger instead. Enos Slaughter led off with a single and stayed on first while Klinger got the next two outs. Harry Walker, who was 6-for-16 in the Series, was up next.

Then came the moment that would soon come to take on a life of its own. Nervous about Walker, Klinger failed to hold Slaughter on first. Slaughter took off for second base as Klinger delivered. Walker stroked a soft hit over Pesky's head at short into center field, where Leon Culberson, in place of DiMaggio, threw kind of a floater to Pesky, the cutoff man. Slaughter was motoring around the diamond; plenty of replays have shown that he was heading for home as Pesky received the ball. His throw would have had to have been perfect and pretty hard to nail Slaughter. Many have said that Pesky hesitated before he made the throw, but that doesn't appear to be the case.

Teammates like Doerr, DiMaggio, and Williams have all came to Pesky's defense after the game and through the years, but it took Pesky many years to live down that infamous moment. Even today Pesky occasionally blames himself, but the loss was more the result of Slaughter's mad dash than Pesky's supposed hesitation.

"The Teammates"—Pesky, Doerr, DiMaggio, and Williams— never got back to a World Series with the Red Sox.

# 55 Red Sox Daddy

Ed Kenney oversaw the Red Sox farm system for almost four decades and watched great players like Carl Yastrzemski, Jim Lonborg, Rico Petrocelli, Carlton Fisk, Jim Rice, Fred Lynn, Wade Boggs, and Roger Clemens develop. But Kenney, who died in 2006, never got the credit or the hoopla he deserved for his accomplishments. He never touted himself as the reason the Sox developed so much talent.

"You never heard him say anything about himself," said his son, Ed Kenney Jr., who took over from his father as the Sox farm director. "He always gave credit to the player or the instructor or the scout. He always believed that he shouldn't take the credit for the development of a player because in the end, it's the player who either makes it or doesn't make it. Dad really cared about these kids, though. I think they loved him like a father."

"He was like a daddy to me," said Dennis "Oil Can" Boyd. "He helped me sort out so many things when I was a young player."

In the early 1990s, late in his Red Sox career, Kenney said, "I just happened to be here, and we had some tremendous scouts. I could fill a book with all the good things that have pleased me. I can go back and recall when some of our minor league players looked as though they would never learn to hit or field. Then all of a sudden, many of them began to smooth out. They became what the scouts said they would."

He always thought the biggest tragedy in baseball is a player who doesn't fulfill his potential. Said Kenney, "When a player with a lot of talent didn't develop because he didn't apply himself, he cheated the Red Sox, and he cheated himself."

According to Kenney, players like Rick Burleson, Boggs, and Ted Williams never cheated themselves. He said Burleson "wasn't a good hitter or runner" when he first came up, but that he turned out to be one of the best shortstops in Red Sox history after a lot of hard work. Kenney, who was employed by the Red Sox since the late 1930s, recalled a young Ted Williams hitting .327, being unhappy with his performance, and then improving to .406 in 1941.

Kenney believed that instructors in the minor league system needed to avoid overdoing it. He always believed that players develop on their own as they mature and that trainers should just get out of the way of that. He believed that every player needs something different, which is why he was a father-like figure to many and a stern taskmaster with others.

# 56 Oh, Pawtucket

The only thing as relaxing as a warm summer night at Fenway is a warm summer night at McCoy Stadium in Pawtucket, home of the Red Sox's Triple A franchise. Call them the crown jewel of minor league baseball. Call them pioneers. But whatever you call them, you can be sure that owner Ben Mondor has made the Pawtucket Red Sox the most recognizable franchise in minor league baseball since he bought the team in 1977, saving the franchise and refurbishing the then-decrepit McCoy Stadium. This is a place Red Sox fans can visit not once, not twice, but a hundred times and never grow tired of the pure Americana, grassroots feel of the place.

In 1981 Pawtucket received national attention when the longest game in the history of professional baseball was played there over two dates. Media from all over the country and other parts of the world witnessed the 33-inning affair.

The first part of the game was played on April 18, 1981, on a 28-degree day; it finished some nine weeks and three days later on June 23 with the temperature at 80 degrees. The game had been suspended after 32 innings, tied 2–2.

Two Hall of Famers played in the game—Sox third baseman Wade Boggs and Cal Ripken Jr.—while Marty Barrett, Bob Ojeda, Bruce Hurst, Rich Gedman, and Mike Boddicker were among the other future major leaguers who were on the PawSox and Rochester rosters at the time. Rochester catcher Dave Huppert caught the first 31 innings in what just happened to be his first game back after injuring a leg sliding into second base a week earlier. The Pawtucket manager was Joe Morgan, who was later responsible for the "Morgan's Magic" era with the big-league team in 1988. Morgan was ejected in the twenty-second inning, watching the next 10 innings of the game through a tiny hole in the back of the dugout.

The seemingly never-ending game wasn't suspended until 4:00 AM. That's because umpire Dennis Cregg and crew chief Jack Lietz's rule book had a page missing: the section on curfews. Mondor brought his copy of the rulebook out to the umpiring crew, showing them that the rule stated that no inning could start after 12:50 AM. Oops! That's when Cregg phoned International League president Harold Cooper at his home in Ohio. Cooper called back shortly after 4:00 AM to inform the crew that they should suspend the game, which they did at 4:07 AM.

"It was a cold, vicious night," recalled team president Mike Tamburro. "We lost a bank of lights before the game started, so we lost about a half hour at the start. I left the ballpark at 5:30 in the morning with the sun rising over the right-field fence. It was Easter Sunday. I went home to change and shower, went to the early Easter

Mass, and drove back here for an afternoon game at 1:00 PM that was tied 2–2 in the ninth. Thank God Sam Bowen hit a home run to win it."

Tamburro recalled that by the time the game was called, 19 fans were left out of the 1,740 who had originally been in attendance that night. Those stalwart few who stayed the course were rewarded with season tickets. Tamburro recalled the flow of people through the ballpark that evening. "People would get off the night shift of the local factories. We had doctors show up from local hospitals. One of them watched the game with Morgan," Tamburro recalled.

"He had just delivered a baby," said Morgan, "and he came over to ask me what I was doing looking through that slot. I said, 'I'm watching the game.' He didn't believe me. So I let him watch and we shared that small opening for a while."

Pawtucket pitcher Luis Aponte, who had pitched four scoreless innings (from the seventh through the tenth innings), got a ride home from Mike Smithson at around 3:30 AM. When he arrived home, Aponte banged on the door to his home; his wife, Xiomara, wouldn't let him in. Aponte told *The Times* of Pawtucket, "My wife won't let me in. She thought I was out drinking all night."

Morgan's wife, Dottie, also called in a panic looking for her husband. "Where are you, Joe?" Mrs. Morgan asked.

"I'm in the clubhouse. We're still playing," said Joe.

Mrs. Morgan: "If you're still playing, why are you in the clubhouse answering the phone?"

Official scorer Bill George's score sheet now rests in Cooperstown. Still, Pawtucket outfielder Chico Walker called it "the most boring game I ever played in." Only four years later, on June 19, 1985, the PawSox and Syracuse engaged in a long affair that was suspended after 22 innings.

But that was a quickie compared to this marathon in '81, which finally ended when Dave Koza lined a sharp single to left field off reliever Chris Speck, driving in Marty Barrett with the winning run in the bottom of the thirty-third inning when the game was resumed on June 23.

# 57 The Songs of the Sox: "Sweet Caroline" and "Tessie"

The ritual of playing "Sweet Caroline" at Fenway at the bottom of the eighth inning has been a Red Sox Nation favorite since 2003. It began in 1998, when a Red Sox employee named his newborn daughter Caroline; the song was played as a tribute to the baby, and a tradition was born as well.

The songwriter, Neil Diamond, told the Associated Press in November 2007 that the inspiration for the 1969 hit song was Caroline Kennedy, John F. Kennedy's daughter. Diamond made the revelation to Kennedy while singing at her 50th birthday party via satellite. Until then, nobody really knew who "Sweet Caroline" was.

Diamond said, "I had never discussed it with anybody before—intentionally. I thought I would tell it to Caroline when I met her someday." Diamond said it was the most significant song of his career, jump-starting his life in the music business. He said he wrote the song after seeing a photo of a young Caroline dressed in riding gear next to her pony.

Red Sox fans never really cared about the origins of the song's title, but knowing that it was about a Kennedy still probably made them smile.

Here are those famous lyrics that Sox fans love to shout:

Where it began
I can't begin to knowin'.
But then I know it's growin' strong.

Was in the spring
And spring became a summer.
Who'd have believed you'd come along.

Hands, touchin' hands,
Reachin' out,
Touchin' me,
Touchin' you.

Sweet Caroline,
Good times never seemed so good.

At that point, fans chant, "So good! So good!"

The song is even played at spring-training games in Fort Myers, Florida. I recall that during one spring-training game in 2006, the song wasn't played at its normal time at the bottom of the eighth, causing many inquisitive fans to look toward the press box, asking, "What happened to 'Sweet Caroline'?" The understandably upset Sox management, realizing what had happened, played the song in the ninth inning, much to the delight of the fans on hand.

"Tessie" was the original song of the Royal Rooters fan club, who used to march into the Huntington Avenue Grounds, former home of the Red Sox, and strum up "Tessie" to get the crowd going. Will R. Anderson wrote the lyrics, which go:

Tessie, you make me feel so badly.
Why don't you turn around?
Tessie, you know I love you madly.
Babe, my heart weighs about a pound.
Don't blame me if I ever doubt you,
You know I wouldn't live without you.
Tessie, you are the only, only, only...

# 58 The Eck

His amazing career landed him as a first-ballot Hall of Famer in 2004. He was a 20-game winner for the Sox in 1978, and he ended his career 20 years later with the Red Sox as a set-up man for Tom Gordon. Dennis Eckersley was a colorful player with long, wavy black hair sticking out of the back of his baseball hat. He invented his own colorful language to describe his pitching, calling his fastball "gas" and his curveball "cheese." He was demonstrative, pumping his fist after striking out a batter.

Eckersley came to the Red Sox from the Indians on March 30, 1978, in a deal the Indians had to make. At the time Eckersley had marital issues; his then-wife Denise had engaged in a much-publicized affair with Indians outfielder Rick Manning. The Red Sox sent Mike Paxton, Bo Diaz, Ted Cox, and veteran Rick Wise to the Indians. In return the Red Sox got an ace for their pitching staff; Eck helped lead them to a tie with the New York Yankees in the pennant race after 162 games in '78. (The Sox proceeded to lose a playoff game to the Yankees, finishing in second place.)

Eckersley went 4–1 against the Yankees in '78. He was 11–1 with a 2.75 ERA at Fenway Park and threw 16 complete games. He won 197 games in his career, saved 390 more, and is one of only two pitchers to win 20 or more and save 50 or more (John Smoltz being the other). However, after a good 1979 campaign with Boston during which he won 17 games and had a 2.99 ERA, Eckersley had four mediocre seasons and was dealt to the Chicago Cubs along with infielder Mike Brumley on May 25, 1984, for Cubs first baseman Bill Buckner.

Eckersley battled alcohol problems in Chicago and eventually entered an alcohol rehabilitation program. He later teamed up with Tony LaRussa in Oakland, who along with pitching coach Dave Duncan had the foresight to convert Eck to the bullpen; he eventually became a closer when Jay Howell was hurt early in the 1987 season.

Eckersley played for so long that he faced both Hank Aaron and Brooks Robinson and was teammates with Carl Yastrzemski, Jim Rice, and Carlton Fisk. While with Oakland he allowed an infamous game-winning homer to Kirk Gibson in Game 1 of the 1988 World Series against the Dodgers. He is now an analyst for the New England Sports Network and remains one of the most popular players in Red Sox history.

# 59 A 17-Run Inning

Boston fans who were around during the summer of 1953 probably weren't paying too much attention to the White Sox. The Korean Conflict was raging and the Sox lineup didn't have Ted Williams, who was off being a war hero as a fighter pilot in the Marines.

Yet on June 18 the Red Sox scored 17 runs against the Tigers in the seventh inning of a 23–3 win; their half of that inning lasted an incredible 47 minutes. There were only 3,108 fans at Fenway that day. The Red Sox sent 23 batters up, and the Tigers used three different pitchers, to no avail. The Red Sox mustered 14 hits (of their 27 that day) and six walks. Gene Stephens, only 20 years old at the time, had three hits (a double and two singles off three different pitchers) in that inning, setting a major league record, and Dick Gernert drove in four of the 17 runs. Catcher Sammy White's three runs tied a major league record for most runs in an inning.

The Red Sox had certainly been involved in high-scoring games and big innings before, given the dimensions of Fenway Park and their rich history of great hitters. But this was a case of pure, unadulterated explosion. The Tigers were a very bad team (although the Sox themselves finished fourth that year).

The Sox led 5–3 heading into the seventh. They peppered Tigers' pitcher Steve Gromek for nine runs, and Dick Weik and Earl Harrist each surrendered four. The Sox had pummeled the Tigers pitching the day before to the tune of a 17–1 win.

Stephens, who had an excellent major league career, played left field in this game as a replacement for Williams, who returned later that season. (Stephens was then optioned back to Triple A Louisville, Kentucky.) Interestingly, another Red Sox player—Johnny Damon—also had three hits in a 14-run first inning; his came in a June 27, 2003, blowout of the Florida Marlins, which the Sox won 25–8.

"It just seemed like everything was a base hit or a walk," Stephens told *The Boston Globe*'s Gordon Edes many years later. "There are two things I remember about the game. I remember the manager for Detroit, one of the greatest guys to ever put on a uniform—Fred Hutchinson, a big ol' burly guy. The other thing I remember, George Kell made two outs in the inning—one to end the inning—and both were line drives. Gosh, it's been so long ago. I got two singles and a double, but there wasn't much made of it at the time."

# 60 The Jimmy Fund

The Jimmy Fund has been an official Red Sox charity since 1953. It was first formed in 1948 by executives and owners of the Boston Braves to raise money for Dr. Sidney Farber's research with the Children's Cancer Research Foundation. Einar Gustafson, the original Jimmy, was selected to speak on Ralph Edwards's national radio program "Truth or Consequences," which was broadcast from the boy's hospital room for his appearance. Gustafson was given the nickname "Jimmy" at the time to protect his anonymity. "Jimmy's" appeal generated more than $200,000 in one year to support Dr. Farber's research—and the Jimmy Fund was born. Gustafson's cancer later went into remission and he lived to be 65 years old, passing away due to a stroke in 2001. The charity, which later became the major fund-raising arm of the Dana Farber Cancer Institute, was inherited by the Red Sox when the Braves left Boston in the early 1950s for Milwaukee.

Ted Williams was one of the most instrumental players in creating awareness for the charity. He befriended Dr. Sidney Farber and through his celebrity helped spread the word about Farber's work in researching children's cancer. For much of his career in Boston, Williams often visited the hospital unannounced and without fanfare to spend time with the children and also attended many fund-raising events on behalf of the hospital. Williams got other players and sports celebrities involved as well.

The other major player involved with the Jimmy Fund was Mike Andrews, the popular second baseman on the Impossible Dream team in 1967, who became the executive director of the Jimmy Fund and has made raising funds for the charity his life's work. Andrews joined the Jimmy Fund after retiring from baseball in 1973. He worked as a volunteer for former Red Sox broadcaster Ken Coleman, who worked as the fund's executive director. Andrews took over as the chairman of the Jimmy Fund in 1979 and still holds the position.

Over the years many Red Sox players have made visits to the hospital to see the children. Mo Vaughn, a popular player for the Sox in the 1990s, was a frequent visitor and did much to help the cause.

The Jimmy Fund has long been associated with the Red Sox, and taking a role in their charity functions has also been a favorite endeavor of Sox fans off the field.

*Einar Gustafson, pictured here in 1998, is the cancer survivor for whom the Jimmy Fund is named. Gustafson's 1948 plea on the radio show "Truth or Consequences"—during which he went by "Jimmy" to protect his anonymity—raised over $200,000 in one year to help with children's cancer research.* Photo courtesy of AP/Wide World Photos.

# 61 Denny Galehouse?

The Red Sox wound up losing a one-game playoff to the Cleveland Indians on October 4, 1948, thanks to a curious decision by manager Joe McCarthy to pitch embattled veteran Denny Galehouse over veteran Ellis Kinder or rookie phenom Mel Parnell.

The Sox wound up losing the game 8–3 as Galehouse was lit up, tagged for an early three-run homer by Cleveland's MVP candidate Lou Boudreau. McCarthy's decision never made much sense, no matter how it was explained. He has said that he wanted to stay away from Parnell because he was a lefty and because Cleveland's offense might come from the right side. Kinder was passed up for no apparent reason. He had won four of his previous five starts and seemed rested. McCarthy seemed focused on the fact that Galehouse had pitched eight and two-thirds innings of brilliant relief against Cleveland on July 30, but he seemed to forget that Galehouse had allowed nine runs over five innings in his most recent outing against Cleveland. In any event, McCarthy wasn't too sure of his decision, keeping it a secret from the media and the Indians until close to game time. Joe Cronin, the team's general manager, confirmed many years later that McCarthy had told catcher Birdie Tebbetts to ask the starting pitchers who wanted to pitch the playoff game, and the only one who raised his hand was Galehouse

Poor Galehouse was roughed up by the media and fans. This was very different from 2003, when Pedro Martinez bore none of the blame when he was left in too long in Game 7 of the ALCS, allowing three runs and squandering a three-run lead to the Yankees. Grady Little took all the blame for that one.

The good news was that the Sox won two games from the Yankees on the final weekend of the '48 season to eliminate New York from pennant contention. The first win, 5–1 behind Jack Kramer, eliminated the Yankees, and the second, a 10–5 victory, enabled the Red Sox to tie the Indians' season record, necessitating a one-game playoff for the American League pennant.

# 62 The Monster Seats

Architect Janet Marie Smith hit a grand slam with this idea. Sometime between now and whenever, you've got to experience the Green Monster seating. For years the Green Monster was a wall and then netting above it to catch home runs. But between the '02 and '03 seasons the Sox plunked 270 seats atop the Green Monster.

Smith, who also designed Camden Yards in Baltimore, said at the time, "The idea for Green Monster seating has been around for years and we were thrilled to be in a position to implement this. We haven't changed the configuration of Fenway. We haven't changed its occupancy, but we've removed some of the standing room only seats. People who were standing in a congested aisle in years past will now have a place to go. We worked hard on the Green Monster seats to make sure they weren't overpowering Fenway, that they didn't overshadow the importance of the Green Monster, either literally or figuratively. We hope the fans feel we struck the right balance."

Indeed they did. The idea was a stroke of brilliance. Suddenly fans were able to watch a game from the top of the Wall looking toward home plate from one of the most unique views in all of sports. Instead of being able to catch a foul ball, fans can catch a home run.

*Fans in the Green Monster seats at Fenway hold up a sign as Barry Bonds of the San Francisco Giants is up to bat against the Boston Red Sox on June 17, 2007.*

Fans who sit there certainly have a great view of those questionable homers—the ones that hit atop the wall but don't necessarily go over. They also have a unique view of the ball bouncing off the wall and, of course, a bird's-eye view of left fielder Manny Ramirez and his quirky behavior. But spectators better pay attention to the game while they're up there. Balls can fly in their direction at an unbelievable speed, and someone who isn't watching could easily get plunked.

And many a spill has shown that keeping a beer cup too close to the edge of the Wall is not a wise idea, either.

# 63 Coup LeRoux

To give some understanding of how strange and wacky the history of the Red Sox ownership has often been, I present Exhibit A: Coup LeRoux.

The late Edward G. "Buddy" LeRoux was actually a pretty good egg. We got to know each other and spoke a lot during and after the time he held his ownership interest in the Red Sox.

June 6, 1983, was supposed to be a feel-good story at Fenway. It was "Tony Conigliaro Night," and Conig and the 1967 Red Sox were being honored. LeRoux, in addition to being part-owner of the team, had been the trainer for the '67 Sox. He was quite successful as a trainer for both the Boston Celtics dynasty and the Red Sox in the '60s; he befriended the Yawkeys and was given a loan of $1 million by Mrs. Yawkey to join her as a general partner along with Haywood Sullivan.

But LeRoux didn't like the way the team was being run by Yawkey and Sullivan, and so he staged what came to be known as "Coup LeRoux." He held a press conference in which he said he was taking control of the team. He announced plans to bring back Dick O'Connell as his general manager. O'Connell had been fired by Mrs. Yawkey in 1977, when the GM's job was given to Sullivan.

LeRoux explained his actions, saying, "The limited partners have become very concerned about the disarray in the general partnership." Sullivan called his own press conference moments later in which he said, "I want to make a correction. The release that you hold before you states the Red Sox announced this reorganization. The Red Sox did not. The announcement was made by Buddy LeRoux. It is illegal, invalid, above all, not effective."

LeRoux claimed the limited partners had reorganized and named him sole managing general partner; he named Judge Samuel Adams as the club's general counsel. Sullivan countered that the two other general partners and the 14 limited partners—including Harold Alfond, Thomas DiBenedetto, H.M. Stevens, Inc., Dr. Arthur Pappas, Samuel Tamposi, and Mrs. Jean Yawkey—"did not agree and some of them didn't even know about this."

LeRoux, who was supposed to be introduced along with the remainder of the '67 squad that night, took himself out of the program. The '67 players were, as a group, incensed that LeRoux would pull his stunt on their night. LeRoux regretted the timing but said that his lawyer had advised him that his actions had to take place that night.

The courts overruled LeRoux, giving control to Yawkey and Sullivan and ordering LeRoux to sell his share of the team, which he eventually did for $7 million. In the end LeRoux's actions completely ruined his reputation as well as his relationship with the Sox. After losing his share of the Sox LeRoux later purchased Suffolk Downs Raceway, which turned out to be a bust as well. The racetrack was never able to get the slot machines LeRoux believed would make him unbelievably rich. Nor did any sports team ever build a new stadium on the property. To make matters worse, horse racing soon became a dying industry.

# 64 Sully

Player, manager, owner—not many men can claim all three titles on their résumé. But Haywood Sullivan did. He was a strong man with strong ideas. He was part of the Yawkey legacy, and then again he wasn't. He was a personal favorite of Thomas Yawkey and later Jean Yawkey and eventually was loaned $1 million by Mrs. Yawkey to buy into the general partnership of the team in 1978. In the years after Mrs. Yawkey's death, Sullivan's conservative approach clashed with John Harrington, who had taken over the Yawkey Estate and had different ideas about how to put a team together. When the Yawkey Estate bought Sullivan out for $12 million, Harrington was given complete control.

Sullivan was very committed to player development. His philosophy was that every five years a team should be able to completely turn over its players with prospects from its farm system, thus eliminating the need to pay high salaries to big-time players in free agency. It was certainly a noble philosophy, and it might have worked in smaller markets, but it was clear that the Red Sox were competing with the high-payroll Yankees, and they needed to keep pace.

Sullivan took over as the team's general manager in 1977 from Dick O'Connell, who was fired by Jean Yawkey shortly after Thomas Yawkey's death. He ran the team as GM until he turned over that aspect of the operation to Lou Gorman in 1984. He fought with general partner Edward "Buddy" LeRoux, who tried to stage a takeover of the team in 1983.

Sullivan, a catcher who played seven seasons for the Red Sox and the Kansas City A's and later managed the A's for a season, is blamed for Carlton Fisk's escape to the Chicago White Sox after the 1980 season; Sullivan failed to send Fisk a contract before the required December 20 deadline. But he overcame that loss by promoting from within and developing top players in the Sox organization.

"I came from nothing," said Sullivan, who had been a great athlete from Dothan, Alabama, and was also a catcher and a quarterback at the University of Florida. He was signed to a then huge $50,000 bonus by the Red Sox, but he never lived up to his billing as a player. He took great pride in his son, Marc, becoming a backup catcher for the Red Sox.

Sullivan was a quiet man who didn't care for the limelight. He rarely spoke publicly, but he was a decent man. He died suddenly in February 2003 in Fort Myers—the city that, with Sullivan's help, had become the Red Sox's spring-training location when they moved from Winter Haven, Florida, in the early 1990s.

# 65 Retired Numbers

Up on the right-field facade of the Fenway grandstand are the numbers 1, 4, 8, 9, 27, and 42. They are the Red Sox's retired numbers, and they belong to Bobby Doerr, Joe Cronin, Carl Yastrzemski, Ted Williams, Carlton Fisk, and Jackie Robinson (although he never played for the Red Sox, his No. 42 was retired nationally). The Red Sox's criteria for retiring numbers is that the player has to be elected to the Hall of Fame and has to have played for at least 10 years with the Red Sox. The Red Sox first started wearing numbers on their uniforms in 1931.

Bobby Doerr, whose number was retired on May 21, 1988, was elected to the Hall of Fame in 1986. Doerr was a .288 career hitter and played his entire career with the Red Sox, from 1937 to 1951. In 1950 he led the American League in triples (along with teammate Dom DiMaggio) with 11. In 1944 he led the American League in slugging percentage with .528. He also hit .409 in the 1946 World Series, going 9-for-22.

Joe Cronin's number was retired on May 29, 1984, and he was elected to the Hall of Fame in 1956. He hit .301 in 20 major league seasons and also won 1,071 games as a manager, the most in Red Sox history, leading Boston to the 1946 pennant as a manager. He also became the American League president, becoming the first ex-player to do so. He holds the American League record for most pinch-hit homers with five in 1943, and that season he became the first player to hit pinch-hit homers in both games of a doubleheader.

Carl Yastrzemski's number was retired on August 6, 1989, and he was elected to the Hall of Fame in 1989, receiving 95 percent of the vote. He was the first player to make it to the Hall of Fame after taking part in the Little League youth baseball program. He won the Triple Crown in 1967 and remains the last player to have done so. He holds the record for games played in the American League with 3,308, and he was the first American League player with more than 400 homers and 3,000 hits. He also won seven Gold Gloves as a left fielder.

Ted Williams was voted a starting outfielder on the Greatest Living Team in 1969. He won two Triple Crowns, six batting titles, and four home-run titles, and he led the league nine times in slugging percentage. He holds the major league record for reaching base on 16 consecutive occurrences. He was the oldest player to win a batting title, going .388 in 1957 at the age of 39, and he then won the title again at age 40 the following year. His number was retired on May 29, 1984.

Carlton Fisk held the record for most home runs by a catcher with 351 until Mike Piazza surpassed him. He's a seven-time All-Star best known for his dramatic twelfth-inning walk-off homer against Cincinnati's Pat Darcy in Game 6 of the 1975 World Series.

# 66 The RemDawg

Jerry Remy is the New England Sports Network (NESN) color commentator, and he is more popular now than he ever was as a

*Jerry Remy's popular hot dog stand, RemDawgs, is clearly visible in this exterior shot of Gate C at Fenway Park.*

player for the Red Sox. He played for Boston for seven years, from 1978 to 1984, after coming in on a trade for Don Aase in the winter of 1977.

Remy owns a popular hot dog stand located right outside of Gate C called Remdawgs; it features large, plump, juicy hot dogs with all the fixings that are often enjoyed by Sox fans right before they go into the game. The neat thing about Remdawgs is that it's located right next to the portable NESN studio where *The Boston Globe* Red Sox pregame show is recorded. Remy, as well as various guests, tape segments for the show in front of hundreds of Red Sox fans who gather around the stage and the hot dog stand to watch the show before entering the ballpark.

Remy is an insightful and rather funny color analyst who partakes in sometimes silly ribbing and joking with play-by-play partner Don Orsillo during Red Sox broadcasts. Remy analyzes the upcoming game or reviews the game played the previous evening with host Tom Caron and a rotating cohost—either former Red Sox pitcher Dennis Eckersley, Red Sox great Jim Rice, or former Pawtucket and Oakland A's manager Ken Macha.

Remy has become one of the best color analysts in the country, usually drawing rave reviews from both local and national TV critics. With his keen insights into the game and in-depth knowledge of Red Sox personnel, he has a knack for being able to anticipate what could happen next with the team.

Remy was raised in Somerset, Massachusetts, and rose quickly through the Angels minor league system. He won the batting title with El Paso in the Texas League, hitting .338, and then went to Triple A Salt Lake City. Remy took the second-base job there from another future Red Sox second baseman, Denny Doyle, in 1975. The funny story here is that he also replaced Doyle when the Red Sox traded for him in 1978.

Remy was a terrific defensive second baseman who had speed and played the game with reckless abandon. Knee injuries slowed him down in 1984, and he retired when it became evident to him that he could no longer play at the level to which he was accustomed.

# 67 Leather

Watching Coco Crisp play center field in 2007, it was hard to imagine that there had ever been better defensive center fielders in Red Sox history—but apparently there were, along with many other defensive stars.

Though I don't pretend to have seen Tris Speaker play or even to have watched a lot of his film, baseball historians agree that he was a pretty special defensive player; he is widely considered the best defensive player the Red Sox ever had. The Hall of Famer played really shallow center field because he was so good at going back on the ball. There are reports that Speaker couldn't have been more than 40 to 50 feet behind the infield. In softball that's called short center field. It might have been the shallowest anybody has played in baseball history.

The Red Sox have had other notable center fielders. For instance, in his prime Fred Lynn made some incredible catches, usually running pretty far to track down the ball. Another great center fielder in the 1970s was Rick Miller, who never got the acclaim he deserved because he wasn't a full-time player. And those who watched Dom DiMaggio thought he was the best in the American League during his days in the 1940s and early 1950s, and when Jimmy Piersall replaced him, Ted Williams commented that "he's the best [defensive] centerfielder I've ever seen."

In the old days, Duffy Lewis got a lot of credit for how he played the left-field embankment known as "Duffy's Cliff." And while there have been very good right fielders, none have been better than Dwight Evans, who won eight Gold Gloves and had one of the strongest throwing arms ever seen. Evans is best known for the tremendous catch he made in Game 6 of the 1975 World Series. He was a player you didn't run on either. Harry Hooper was also an excellent right fielder, as was Jackie Jensen in the 1950s.

Yaz, a seven-time Gold Glove winner in left field, was likely the best modern-day outfielder the Red Sox ever had. Aside from that incredible somersaulting catch off Yankees outfielder Tom Tresh to preserve Billy Rohr's no-hit bid in April 1967 at Yankee Stadium, he was consistently amazing in left with one highlight-reel-worthy catch after another. He learned to play the left-field wall as well as anyone, often holding batters to singles.

Another special defender was first baseman George "Boomer" Scott. He simply had a natural affinity for the position. He scooped up some terrible throws that had no business being caught, and he made some terrific plays around the bag on balls that should have been base hits. Some, like Carl Yastrzemski, considered him to be a first-base version of Brooks Robinson, so fluid and natural that he made hard plays look easy. And while Kevin Youkilis isn't the slick fielder that Boomer was, in '07 he went without making an error in the regular season to break the American League record for error-less games.

Over at the hot corner Frank Malzone won three Gold Gloves before Brooks Robinson came along to retire that award. Malzone was one of the most fundamentally sound third basemen of his generation. Wade Boggs, on the other hand, was an underrated third baseman. While he never won a Gold Glove for Boston, he won two with the Yankees after he left. Current third baseman Mike Lowell is also considered one of the best with one Gold Glove in his trophy case.

The consistency of Bobby Doerr at second base is unparalleled. Sadly, the Red Sox have never really had a " vacuum cleaner" shortstop over the long term. But behind the plate, Carlton Fisk was one of the great all-around catchers ever, and Jason Varitek, who has also won a Gold Glove, is considered one of the best game callers in Sox history.

# 68 They Called the Shots

With all due respect to the great Red Sox announcers who have come and gone, my all-time favorite was Ned Martin. He not only announced the game, he also told the story of the game at the same time. "Mercy!" was his favorite expression, and he would use it only to explain the best or the worst of anything. When he used it, fans knew something very good or something very bad had just happened.

Martin's voice was soothing and mellow, almost poetic. He was like a writer speaking about the game. He was heard over the airwaves on both radio and TV from 1961 to 1992, making him the longest-tenured Sox broadcaster. During his career he teamed up with two other legends, Hall of Famer Curt Gowdy and longtime Sox broadcaster Ken Coleman (whom he worked with from 1966 to 1972 on both radio and TV). Martin called the 1967 World Series on the radio and the 1975 World Series for NBC-TV. He called the pop-up to Rico Petrocelli that clinched the 1967 pennant and is also known for his call of Roger Clemens's 20-strikeout game in 1986.

Martin loved to talk about the game away from the mike as well. He also loved the ocean, often visiting Laguna Beach with Coleman. Martin died on July 23, 2002, after attending a tribute to the late Ted Williams. He was perfectly eulogized by former *Globe* TV columnist Bill Griffith, who said, "Long before there was

Morgan's Magic on the field in 1988, there was Martin's Magic on the radio."

Another superb play-by-play man and personal favorite of mine was Sean McDonough, who succeeded Martin in 1988. McDonough adored Martin and adopted much of his style after years of listening to him.

Gowdy, who had a folksier style, was teamed with Bob Murphy before Martin's arrival. Gowdy called Williams's final at-bat on September 28, 1960. "Everybody quiet now here at Fenway Park after they gave him a standing ovation of two minutes, knowing that this is probably his last time at bat," Gowdy said. "One out, nobody on, last of the eighth inning. Jack Fisher into his windup, here's the pitch. Williams swings and there's a long drive to deep right! The ball is going and it is gone! A home run for Ted Williams in his last time at bat in the major leagues!" Gowdy went off in 1966 to become one the first superstar broadcasters for NBC. He also hosted the popular *American Sportsman* series.

Coleman had two stints with the Red Sox totaling 20 years. I'll never forget his call of Carl Yastrzemski's catch off Tom Tresh to preserve Billy Rohr's no-hitter on April 14, 1967: "Fly ball, left field...Yastrzemski is going hard.... Way back...way back...and he dives and makes a tremendous catch. One of the greatest catches I've ever seen!" said Coleman on WHDH-TV in Boston.

In 2007 Joe Castiglione completed his 25th season as the Red Sox's radio voice. He spent 14 years with Jerry Trupiano, but in '07 the Sox added Dave O'Brien, a superb announcer who does many ESPN games, and Glenn Geffner, who had been the Red Sox's director of public relations. Castiglione has called two championship-clinching games. In '04, when the Sox ended their 86-year curse, his call was: "Swing and a ground ball, stabbed by [Keith] Foulke. He has it. He underhands to first, and the Boston Red Sox are the world champions! For the first time in 86 years, the Red Sox have won baseball's world championship! Can you believe it?"

Former Red Sox players Johnny Pesky, Mel Parnell, Bob Montgomery, Mike Andrews, and Rico Petrocelli, among others, have all also spent time in the Sox radio and TV booths doing color commentary over the years.

# 69 Soup's On

In a 64-page ruling handed down on December 23, 1975, arbitrator Peter Seitz ruled in favor of Andy Messersmith and Dave McNally, who had challenged baseball's reserve clause, setting the wheels in motion for mass free agency. The Red Sox, with Haywood Sullivan in charge now that Thomas Yawkey had recently passed away, certainly didn't like to spend money. Nonetheless, they decided to make a splash, if for no other reason than to keep up with their competition. They offered Minnesota's Bill "Soup" Campbell a five-year, $1 million contract, which he accepted on November 6, 1976. Campbell, who had gone 17–5 with 20 saves for the Minnesota Twins in 1976, accepted the deal, commenting at his introductory press conference that, "No one's worth that, but if they want to pay me, I'm certainly not going to turn it down."

Campbell wanted a raise in Minnesota after his great season, but tightwad Twins owner Calvin Griffith wasn't about to dish out that kind of money. So Campbell became a free agent. The Sox were definitely in need of a closer. They were using Jim Willoughby in that role in a bullpen that also had Tom Murphy, Tom House, Reggie Cleveland, and Dick Pole.

Campbell proved himself to be worth every penny during his first season. In 69 games and 140 innings, Campbell was 13–9 with a 2.96 ERA. He saved an American League–leading 31 games for

Don Zimmer's team, but it was evident even then that Zimmer was like a little kid with a new toy: he used it until it broke. Campbell's elbow began acting up, and for the remaining four years of his contract he was limited with his innings and appearances. He never again pitched more than 54 innings in a Sox uniform.

The pattern was obvious in '77. Twice Zimmer used him for four straight days. In August he pitched eight times in a 10-day span. In 1978 Campbell was able to make only nine appearances after July 24, and it became painfully obvious that the Sox's first big free-agent purchase was damaged goods. Campbell pitched in major league baseball until he was 38 years old but never regained the form he had had in 1976.

# 70 Deal or No Deal?

Red Sox fans had to be pretty excited on June 15, 1976, when Boston purchased star outfielder Joe Rudi and star closer Rollie Fingers from Oakland A's owner Charles O. Finley for $1 million apiece. Finley had also sold off star lefty Vida Blue to the Yankees for $1 million.

Rudi had been instrumental in the three Oakland championships. He made a huge catch off Dennis Menke in the 1972 World Series, and in 1974 he hit the Series-clinching homer against Mike Marshall. After the '74 Series he finished second in the MVP voting behind Jeff Burroughs. Dick Williams once called him "the best goddamn winning baseball player around."

Sox manager Darrell Johnson really liked Rudi's game, and they also shared a love of hunting. When Finley approached Dick O'Connell about which A's players he might want to acquire,

*Red Sox fans were excited about the June 15, 1976, acquisition of Joe Rudi, pictured here on June 16, 1976 (notice the Red Sox uniform). The day after this photo was taken, commissioner Bowie Kuhn voided the sale, and Rudi ended up signing with the Angels.* Photo courtesy of AP/Wide World Photos.

O'Connell asked Johnson, who told him Rudi and Fingers. Sox assistant GM John Claiborne flew to Oakland to meet with both players and see what it would take to sign them to long-term contracts. Both of their deals were up, and with free agency finally a reality, there was no way Finley was going to pay them what they were worth. He seemed astoundingly content to break up a team that had won three championships.

Claiborne realized after his meeting that he could probably lock up both players, and the sale was made. From a phone booth in Oakland, Rudi and Fingers immediately called their agent, Jerry Kapstein, to ask what they should do. "I advised them to report," Kapstein recalled. "I know that Joe, being from the Bay Area, had mixed emotions about going. Rollie Fingers was also stunned by the turn of events. I told them it was their duty to report to Boston as soon as they could and then wait to see how things unfolded."

The players showed up. Rudi put on his No. 28 Sox jersey and Fingers his No. 34, although Johnson didn't use either that night. The next day word came down that Commissioner Bowie Kuhn was in the process of making a decision regarding the sale, and on June 18 Kuhn voided the deals "in the best interests of baseball." Rudi and Fingers went back to Oakland, where Finley banned them from the ballpark for two weeks before they were allowed back. Rudi wound up signing with the Angels after the season. Fingers went on to a Hall of Fame career.

Still disappointed about not securing Rudi, the Sox swung a trade with the Angels to sign him in January 1981, although by then he was far past his prime. They also got Frank Tanana and Jim Dorsey in the deal in exchange for Fred Lynn and Steve Renko. "This time, it's for real," Rudi told Peter Gammons of *The Boston Globe*.

# 71 Bruno's Catch

Now *this* is when those undesirable seats in the right-field corner at Fenway come in handy. The cameras didn't really pick it up, but Tom Brunansky caught the ball. It was a twisting liner to right by Chicago White Sox shortstop Ozzie Guillen with two on and two out in the top of the ninth in the final game of the 1990 season—a game the Red Sox had to win, and they were leading, 3–1. Brunansky ran with reckless abandon toward the right-field wall, making a fantastic diving catch.

First-base umpire Tim McClelland didn't make the call right away because a fan had jumped out of the stands and blocked his view. Fans swarmed the field. Brunansky, who also had a big run-scoring triple in a three-run Boston second inning off White Sox starter Alex Fernandez, actually realized his cap was missing and went back to get it, but many of us thought Brunansky went back to get the ball.

With that catch—the final out of the final game of the 1990 regular season at Fenway—the Red Sox won the American League East title.

"I saw the play," said McClelland later. "He never dropped the ball."

Good thing. Sitting in the press box that night, I couldn't see at all whether Brunansky made the catch or not. I was just going by the reactions of the fans sitting in that corner of the field.

This was one of the great games of the 1990s at Fenway. Mike Boddicker pitched a gem for seven innings until Jeff Reardon came on for the final two. In the ninth, Sammy Sosa stroked a single up the middle and moved to second when Reardon hit Scott Fletcher with a pitch. That brought up Guillen, who manager Joe Morgan called "the smartest player in baseball." Well, Guillen was about to prove Morgan's point. He hit that twisting liner, which certainly looked as if: 1) it would drop in; and 2) if it did fall, it would be a hit that could get by Brunansky.

Thankfully, neither of those outcomes came to be.

"When you're a kid learning to play the outfield, you're taught to make a quick reaction. That's what I did. When I saw the ball, I went right to it. No hesitation. No time to think about what I should be doing. I just had to do it," Brunansky explained.

Brunansky flipped the ball to McClelland after the out. After the game McClelland walked into the Sox clubhouse and gave it to Brunansky.

Guillen has said that before the ninth inning started he told his teammates, "If I got a chance to hit, I'll tie the game." Guillen fouled off one pitch and then Red Sox catcher Tony Pena turned to Guillen and said, "Don't screw this game up for us."

Boddicker, who had been acquired by the Sox in July 1988, finished the season at 17–8 and was 39–22 with the Red Sox for a winning percentage of .639. During the same time period Roger Clemens's winning percentage was .630 (41–24).

The win, coupled with a Toronto loss, allowed the Sox to win the East by two games. They won six out of their last eight games and headed into the playoffs feeling pretty good about themselves.

# 72 Young Bucks: Red Sox Rookies of the Year

How could a player start his career any better than Walt Dropo did in 1950? The Sox thought they had the second coming of Jimmie Foxx. He was 6'5" and 220 pounds of muscle. The big right-handed-hitting first baseman was 27 years old when he came up from the minors, but it was worth the wait. Dropo led the American League with 144 RBIs and 326 total bases that year. He hit .322 with 34 home runs, behind Cleveland's Al Rosen. He had an OPS of .961, which was third overall. He was named to the All-Star team as well. Dropo never had a year quite like that again. He broke his wrist in 1951 and never fully recovered or regained the great stroke he once had.

Like Dropo, Don Schwall never had a better season than his 1961 rookie year. He went 15–7 and had a 3.22 ERA on a bad team. The big right-hander won his first five decisions and started 13–2. He also pitched three innings of the 1961 All-Star Game at Fenway Park, which ended in a 1–1 tie when rain stopped the game in the ninth inning. Schwall went 9–15 the following season and was sent to Pittsburgh along with catcher Jim Pagliaroni for first baseman Dick Stuart and right-handed pitcher Jack Lamabe. Schwall also worked as a reliever over a seven-year career during which he had a 48–47 record.

After short stints in 1969 and 1971, Carlton Fisk came up for good in '72 and didn't leave the game until 1993. His Hall of Fame career started by winning not only Rookie of the Year but also a Gold Glove—which is very difficult for a rookie player to do—despite making 15 errors. He hit .293 with 22 homers and 61 RBIs as well.

Fred Lynn was Rookie of the Year *and* Most Valuable Player in 1975, becoming the first player to ever win both titles in the same season. Not bad for starters. This enormously gifted center fielder had Boston fans tickled to think they had the game's best young player smack in the middle of their lineup. Add fellow rookie Jim Rice and you had two of the best young players in the game hitting back-to-back. Lynn hit .331 and led the American League in doubles, runs, and slugging. He also won the Gold Glove and was known for his great running catches.

Even as a rookie in 1997, Nomar Garciaparra was so good that the Red Sox moved established shortstop John Valentin to second base and then to third to accommodate him. In 1997 he hit 30 homers and knocked in 98 runs, a major league record for a leadoff hitter. During the course of his first full season he amassed a 30-game hitting streak, and there was talk that he might surpass Dom DiMaggio's Sox record of 34 straight games. Having an emerging star at shortstop excited Red Sox Nation, as Boston had always struggled at that position over the years. He won batting titles in 1999 and 2000 with .357 and .372 batting averages, becoming the first right-handed hitter to do so since Joe DiMaggio. Garciaparra, Alex Rodriguez, and Derek Jeter came to be known as "the Holy Trinity of shortstops."

Diminutive second baseman Dustin Pedroia came a long way from the .172 average he possessed on May 1 to become the overwhelming choice for Rookie of the Year in 2007. Pedroia, a former Arizona State University shortstop, surprised all of his critics, who said he was too small and had too big of a swing to be successful in the major leagues. He hit .317 with a .380 on-base percentage and became one of the league's better defensive second basemen, making the transition from shortstop seamlessly. Pedroia also hit .283 in 14 postseason games in 2007 and was part of Boston's 2007 World Series championship team.

# 73 Red Sox Nation Road Trips

It's tough to get tickets at Fenway. Everybody wants them. It's often easier to just take your Red Sox fandom on the road. As a journalist who travels a lot with the Red Sox and covers other baseball stories nationally, the number of Red Sox fans I see whereever I go never ceases to amaze me. The common theme seems to be, "I can't get tickets to a Red Sox game at Fenway, so I might as well go on the road, where there are plenty of tickets and the prices are lower."

For instance, it's amazing to see the number of Red Sox fans at Tropicana Field, home of the Tampa Bay Devil Rays, when the Red Sox come to town. It might as well be a home game.

"Our fans are amazing," said Sox third baseman Mike Lowell. "You don't see this anywhere else. I suppose there are New Yorkers who watch the Yankees on the road just like us, but there's nothing like going to a road ballpark and seeing so many Red Sox fans in the stands and cheering for you, and at times overshadowing the fans from that town. I could see where that would be a little deflating and humiliating for the home team."

Indeed. Camden Yards in Baltimore, which was once packed to the brim with Orioles fans, has seen spectators staying away in droves while the team struggles to rebuild their franchise. In the meantime, there are plenty of empty seats. When the Sox play there, at least half of the seating, sometimes more, is occupied by Red Sox fans drowning out the home crowd. They get to tour the Inner Harbor, with all of its shops and restaurants, and then take in a game at one of the most beautiful ballparks in baseball. Afterward there are plenty of bars in the area to keep fans busy late at night.

Similar scenarios can be seen in Toronto at the Rogers Centre, in Chicago at U.S. Cellular Field, and as far west as Anaheim and Oakland. Red Sox Nation travels everywhere. Many Boston fans live in New York, and because Yankee Stadium's capacity is so big (57,545), there's a healthy element of Sox fans even there. They playfully chant "Yankees Suck!" when and if the Red Sox get the better of the men in pinstripes.

Sometimes the majority of aircrafts to Tampa or Baltimore or Toronto or New York are filled with Red Sox fans going to the game or spending a weekend in the city the Red Sox are playing in and then trying to catch a peek at their beloved stars at the team hotel.

In many ways it's a better opportunity for Sox fans to bond with their favorite players, and it's somewhat easier to get an autograph.

"I don't think any team has fans like this," said David Ortiz. "When we go on the road, we never feel like we're on the road."

# 74 Crazy Like a Foxx

The funniest line I ever read about Jimmie Foxx was said by New York Yankees pitcher Lefty Gomez, who quipped, "He has muscles in his hair." Foxx spent only six of his 20 years in baseball in Boston, so the Red Sox can't claim him as a career man (although he did choose the Boston cap when he was inducted into the Hall of Fame in 1951). But what an influential six seasons they were.

The hard-hitting first baseman from Sudlersville, Maryland, reached the 500-home-run mark by age 32 and 336 days; he is the second-youngest player (after Alex Rodriguez) to do so. He came to Boston when Connie Mack, who ran the Philadelphia A's, sold him to the Sox for $150,000 and two players after the two couldn't agree on a contract. It's one of the best investments the Red Sox ever made.

There aren't many years like '38. That's when Foxx hit 50 homers, knocked in 175 runs, hit .349, and won the American League MVP. Foxx held that single-season team home-run record until David Ortiz hit 54 in 2006.

We're talking about a guy who hit .360 the following season. We're talking about a hitter who spent 20 years in the majors and had a .325 career average, a .428 on-base percentage, and 1.037 OPS. Here's a slugger who hit 534 homers and knocked in 1,922

*Jimmie Foxx (left) and Ted Williams of the Boston Red Sox pose with their bats on the steps of the dugout. Foxx enjoyed several fantastic years with the Red Sox, particularly his unbelievable 1938 season.*

runs. He won three Most Valuable Player Awards and took the Triple Crown in 1933 with the A's.

That amazing 1938 season wasn't even his best. In 1932, when he won the MVP, he hit 58 homers and knocked in 169 runs. In '33, when he took the Triple Crown, he hit .356 with 48 homers and 163 RBIs.

Foxx drew many comparisons to Babe Ruth—some even called him the right-handed Ruth—because of his absolute dominance at the plate and his ability to hit tape-measure home runs. He ended his career as a pretty good right-handed pitcher, hurling 22⅔ innings in 1945 and allowing four earned runs for a 1.59 ERA.

Foxx became a manager after his playing days, and he skippered the Fort Wayne Daisies of the All-American Girls Professional Softball League. In fact the Tom Hanks character in the movie *A League of Their Own* is loosely based on Foxx. He died in Miami in 1967 at age 59, choking on a bone.

# 75 Hope Springs Eternal

One of the most enjoyable aspects of a sportswriter's job is fleeing the cold of New England in mid-February and heading to Fort Myers, Florida, the winter home of the Red Sox. Evidently, Red Sox Nation feels the same way. The city has grown immensely since the Red Sox first opened their downtown City of Palms Park facility in 1992.

Sox fans have retired there. They have bought second homes. They come in droves in February and March on school vacations, work vacations—you name it—not only to get some warmth in their bones but also to get an early glimpse of the Sox and perhaps watch a new player or two who might have been acquired in the off-season.

It is often the most optimistic part of the baseball season. The pressure is nil. The atmosphere is laid back. For the first two weeks or so there are no games, so players just go through normal workouts and work on fundamentals while pitchers begin to work on their arm strength to build up to their first spring-training outings.

It's been a Sox tradition over the past few years to tip off the spring-training season against Boston College and Northeastern University before getting into the meat of their Grapefruit League schedule. Boston's big spring-training rival is the Minnesota Twins, who play across town at Hammond Stadium, a Lee County facility. Because the teams are located in the same area, they play one another several times each spring, vying for the Lee County Mayors' Cup.

One of the great things about spring training is that it gives fans a chance to get to know players on a more intimate basis. There are more one-on-one, face-to-face meetings with Red Sox players, and fans can follow the development of a player from start to finish while he prepares for the season.

There are always news events happening as well. It used to be, "When will Roger [Clemens] arrive?" Then it became, "When will Pedro [Martinez] come to camp?" Media and fans alike watch excitedly for Manny Ramirez's arrival, especially following an off-season during which he'd demanded to be traded and wasn't. In '07 there was great anticipation of Daisuke Matsuzaka's debut in Fort Myers. It drew hundreds of media from Japan and all around the country. Fort Myers was jam-packed in anticipation.

It's no secret that Sox tickets are hard to come by, and the same holds true for spring-training games. There have been times when fans have camped outside the ballpark for the chance to purchase the few remaining tickets—especially when it comes to Red Sox–Yankees games.

# 76 The Worst There Ever Was

The 1932 Red Sox were clearly the worst team Boston ever fielded. This assortment of journeymen under Shano Collins finished 43–111—a .279 winning percentage—64 games behind the first-place Yankees. Collins actually quit after getting the team off to an 11–44 start; he was replaced by Marty McManus, who didn't fare much better.

How bad was this team? They scored 566 runs, which was 101 fewer than the next worst team, the Chicago White Sox. They hit .251 when the league average was .277. Yeah, but could they pitch? Not really. They had a 5.94 ERA, dead last, while the Yanks had a 4.64. They hit only 53 homers and had a team on-base percentage of .312. Could they run? Not quite. They stole 46 bases and were caught 46 times on attempts. There wasn't a whole lot this team *could* do.

One of them could apparently swim, though. In 1932 Ed Morris, a 19-game winner in 1928, tried to elude an attacker by jumping into the Perdido River in Florida; he swam from the Florida side of the river to Alabama with a knife wound. Although the story sounds kind of funny, it has a tragic ending: Morris caught an infection that killed him.

A few of the Red Sox players did somehow manage to have a halfway decent year. Dale Alexander, who had been acquired from the Tigers along with outfielder Roy Johnson in exchange for Earl Webb, hit .372 with eight homers and 56 RBIs with a .454 on-base percentage. Outfielder Smead Jolley, another Tigers acquisition who came in exchange for Jack Rothrock and catcher Charlie Berry, hit .309 with 18 homers and 99 RBIs. But both players were horrible defensively. Jolley made Manny Ramirez's follies in left field seem tame by comparison. The only starting pitcher for Boston with a winning record that year was Ivy Andrews, who went 8–6.

The city was in the midst of the Great Depression in more ways than one. The Sox drew only 182,150 spectators that miserable season. It was a team of no stars and no hope—except for the fact that Thomas A. Yawkey would come along a year later to buy the team.

# 77 The Old Baby Bull

"Oh, I loved Boston," said Orlando Cepeda when I saw him during the Barry Bonds home-run chase in San Francisco in August 2007. "That was one of the funnest times of my life. That was a great place to play. I loved the city and the fans. It reminded me of San Francisco quite a bit."

On April 6, 1973, Cepeda made his Red Sox debut as the team's first designated hitter. The Sox were home that day, playing against the Yankees; because Ron Blomberg batted in the top of the inning for the Yankees, he became the first designated hitter to ever bat in a game. Cepeda was thus the second designated hitter in major league history, but he did win the first Designated Hitter of the Year award.

Gimpy-legged and barely able to run anymore after multiple knee injuries, Cepeda hit .289 in 1973 with 20 homers, 86 RBIs, and 25 doubles. It was painful at times to watch him run to second on one of his doubles. "It was hard, but I could still hit and I felt that I could still help the team," said Cepeda. "I think I had a good year. I helped us win some games."

Cepeda's performance was streaky that season. During one 11-game stretch from April 18 to May 2 he went 22-for-47 with five homers and 14 RBIs to raise his average from .120 to .347. He dipped over and under the .300 mark but finally ended his Sox career 6-for-40.

Struggling with his legs, as well as new manager Darrell Johnson's desire for a younger team, Cepeda was not re-signed (on Johnson's recommendation), ending his career in Kansas City the following season. He was inducted into the Hall of Fame by the Veterans Committee in 1999. During his career he hit .297 with 379 homers. He was the 1958 National League rookie of the year and won the National League MVP award in 1967.

The Sox finished second in '73 with an 89–63 record, eight games behind Baltimore. It was a disappointing year in that it was a veteran team that had been built to win. Starting shortstop Luis Aparacio, at age 39, hit .271. The Sox did get good pitching performances out of Luis Tiant, who went 20–13, Bill Lee, who was 17–11, and young Rogelio Moret, who went 13–2 with a 3.17 ERA. Tommy Harper, the starting left fielder and leadoff man, also had a good year, stealing a team-record 54 bases.

# 78 The Blame Game

Hall of Fame shortstop Luis Aparicio was 38 years old in 1972, the year he slipped and fell near third base with three games left in the season, costing the Sox a chance to win the American League East division. But was the loss really Aparicio's fault?

The Great Stumble occurred in the third inning, when Carl Yastrzemski sent a long drive off a pitch from Detroit Tiger lefty Mickey Lolich; the ball went over Mickey Stanley's head in center field and hit a bar on the wall above Stanley's head, bouncing behind him. Tommy Harper scored easily, but Yastrzemski, coming in for the second run, was running hard with his head down. He later admitted to thinking, "I've got an inside-the-park home run easy." But when he finally looked up as he rounded second, he saw Aparicio sprawled on the ground past third base. The little shortstop had slipped, and as he tried to get back up Yastrzemski yelled, "Go home! Go home!" But Aparicio went back to third, forcing Yaz to try to get back to second base, where he was tagged out.

While the run scored by Harper off Yaz's single tied the score 1–1, the play took the Sox out of a big inning, and they wound up losing 4–1 before 51, 518 fans that October 2 night.

The Sox had entered the final series of '72 at Tiger Stadium a half game up in the standings. The loss put them a half game back. The next night, with Luis Tiant on the mound, the Sox had a good chance of regaining their lead, but they were bested by Woodie Fryman. Hall of Fame right fielder Al Kaline drove Dick McAuliffe home with the winning run in the seventh, and the Tigers clinched the divisional title with one meaningless game left in the season.

Aparicio was always blamed for the base-running mistake, but many believed the fault truly lay with Yaz. His failure to see the play in front of him cost the Sox a chance to have the tying runs on base. Harper also thought the blame belonged more in Yaz's corner. The shortstop had slipped at third because of some water buildup around the bag; it was Yastrzemski who made a fundamental base-running error. Harper, one of the great base runners of his day, said, "Luis got all the blame, but if you understand good base running, there was a lot more going on there than Luis slipping and falling."

# 79 The Rifleman

In terms of pure arm strength, no one had a stronger gun than Dwight Evans. Base runners feared him, and if there was any doubt as to whether they could make it from first to third, it was erased quickly when Evans would field the ball and gun it toward second base. Evans came up to the Red Sox as a 20-year-old rookie in September 1972 after he'd hit .300 in 144 games at Louisville, Boston's Triple A affiliate at the time.

Evans saw it all. He watched the heartbreaking end of the '72 season, when Luis Aparacio stumbled near third. He made one of the greatest running catches in World Series history during the eleventh inning of Game 6 in 1975, roving in to the right-field corner toward Pesky's Pole to rob Joe Morgan of a home run. Adding insult to injury, he then turned and doubled Ken Griffey off first base to set the stage for Carlton Fisk's walk-off homer in the twelfth.

He was there in 1978 for the devastating playoff loss to the Yankees, though he only pinch hit because he was suffering from the effects of being beaned by a Mike Parrott pitch earlier. He was there in 1986 when the ball went through Bill Buckner's legs. And he was there in 1988 and 1990 when the Sox won their division but bowed out quickly to Oakland in the playoffs.

Evans wound up playing for 20 seasons, 19 of them with the Red Sox and one at the end with the Baltimore Orioles. He won eight Gold Gloves, hit 385 home runs, and batted .272 for his career, hitting in all nine spots in the batting order. He spent the most time as the number two hitter, with 2,534 plate appearances at that spot in the lineup, but he spent significant time everywhere:

leadoff (677 plate appearances), third (910), fourth (595), fifth (1,318), sixth (1,731), seventh (1,267), eighth (1,103), and ninth (434).

Hitting never came naturally to him, however, and he toyed with a hundred different stances. But despite his struggles at the plate, Evans was always a formidable hitter and a tough out. He battled the pitcher every step of the way and he had some big hits. After being beaned by Parrott, he went to work trying to change his swing once and for all to create a better balance at the plate. He worked with hitting guru Walt Hriniak in the early 1980s; Hriniak transformed Evans into a fairly consistent run producer. He was 15 years into his career in 1989 when he finally hit over .300 (.305) in what was his best season, with 34 homers, 123 RBIs, and a .417 on-base percentage.

Evans fell short of being voted into the Hall of Fame, but he was very close. He had a long, productive career; in an era of great right fielders like Dave Winfield and Jesse Barfield, Evans was at the top. While he never quite attained the level of Al Kaline—as many thought he would—he was an excellent player.

In the days when Evans was in right, Fred Lynn was in center, and Yaz was in left, there was no better outfield in the game.

# 80 Clemens Versus Cooney

It was one of the ugliest moments in Red Sox history. Sox ace Roger Clemens was ejected from Game 4 of the 1990 American League Championship Series against Oakland in the second inning of a 3–1 loss to Dave Stewart. The Red Sox were swept.

*One of the ugliest moments in Red Sox history. Roger Clemens was ejected from Game 4 of the 1990 American League Championship Series because of this verbal altercation with home-plate umpire Terry Cooney.* Photo courtesy of AP/Wide World Photos.

It was a Wednesday afternoon on October 10 when Clemens, wearing eye-black and Ninja Turtles shoelaces on his shoes, got into a verbal altercation with home-plate umpire Terry Cooney. The second inning had begun when Carney Lansford singled with one out and got to third on a Terry Steinbach single to left field. Mark McGwire's fielder's choice scored one run, and with two outs, A's second baseman Willie Randolph came up. After walking Randolph—putting runners at first and second after the A's had taken a 1–0 lead—Clemens was shaking his head near the mound and kicking dirt, obviously upset that a couple of pitches hadn't gone his way.

"I was looking down," recalled Clemens after the game. "I saw his [Cooney's] throat guard moving, so he was saying something. He thought I was talking to him. I told him, 'I'm not shaking my f*cking head at you. The problem was not with you.'"

According to players on the field Clemens had used a few obscenities to describe his thoughts concerning one of his pitches and then directed more profanities directly at Cooney. This was an awful display, but even before the incident Clemens just didn't seem to have it that day.

"Roger must have a good idea of his importance to the club," Stewart said. "It's a big game to get kicked out of. I can't imagine what he was thinking. The umpires had a good strike zone both ways."

Cooney has said that Clemens looked disgusted about his last two pitches to Randolph. According to Cooney's account of the incident, when he refused to take his mask off, Clemens spit out a couple of expletives and Cooney threw him out. Clemens ran toward Cooney when he realized he'd been tossed. Umpire Jim Evans came over from right field to restrain Clemens and was shoved by the pitcher. Manager Joe Morgan complained that Clemens should have been warned first before being tossed in such an important game.

The strange day didn't end with the ejection. Second baseman Marty Barrett tossed two buckets of Gatorade and a box of sunflower seeds and gum onto the field to protest the ejection and he, too, was ejected. When coach Dick Berardino tried to settle Barrett down, the second baseman shoved the coach down the dugout steps.

Clemens stayed in the dugout for the rest of the inning and then Evans went over to tell him to leave. "I was watching my team in the playoffs," said Clemens. "Evans told me to leave and I did." Bizarre.

Tom Bolton relieved Clemens, allowing a two-run double to Mike Gallego, making it 3–0. Stewart ran his record against Clemens to 8–0 after the win. He had also beaten Clemens in Game 1 of the Series.

# 81 Joe Cronin

Would the moniker "Mr. Baseball" be too strong? Would it be an inaccurate way to portray the life and times of Joe Cronin? Probably not. He was a player, a player/manger, a manager, a general manager, and the American League president during his long career in baseball.

As he was dying of cancer, Cronin told the late Will McDonough, "I have had a wonderful life. I wouldn't change a thing. I'm the luckiest guy I know. How many people ever got to do just what they wanted to do their whole life?" Joe Cronin apparently did. The Hall of Famer's No. 4 is hung on the right-field facade at Fenway.

Cronin was a career .301 hitter and was considered the best Red Sox shortstop ever. His association with the Red Sox as a player and manager lasted from 1935 to 1947. Cronin was the manager when Ted Williams broke into the majors in 1939, and he later became the general manager. He was inducted into the Hall of Fame in 1956 and served as American League president until he retired in 1973.

You might even say that Cronin was the one to first spawn the vitriol between the Red Sox and the Yankees. In the first game of a doubleheader on May 30, 1938, before 83,533 spectators at Yankee Stadium, Yankees hothead Jake Powell felt Sox pitcher Archie McKain had thrown at him, so Powell charged the mound. Cronin, who was playing shortstop, intercepted Powell's charge and they began to fight, emptying both benches. Both Powell and Cronin were ejected from the game. Cronin had to go through the Yankees' dugout to get back to the visitors' clubhouse. On the way he challenged the entire Yankees team to a fight. They all piled on Cronin, but he handled himself well before his Sox teammates and umpire Cal Hubbard came to his rescue.

After his playing and managing days were over, Cronin admitted how much he loved to beat the Yankees.

Cronin was a compassionate man who always tried to help others. As the GM in 1952 he repeatedly had to deal with the ugly and bizarre behavior of center fielder Jimmy Piersall, who was suffering from a mental illness. (Piersall's breakdown is discussed in more detail later in this book.) Cronin made sure Piersall got help.

Having been around so many players as a teammate, manager, and GM, Cronin was a natural choice to compile an all-time Sox team. Here's what he came up with when asked to pick his "All-Cronin team" in 1982 by *The Globe's* Neil Singelais:

Catcher: Birdie Tebbetts
First base: Jimmie Foxx
Second base: Bobby Doerr
Third base: Frank Malzone

Shortstop: Johnny Pesky
Outfield: Ted Williams, Carl Yastrzemski, and Dom DiMaggio
Right-handed pitcher: Tex Hughson
Left-handed pitcher: Lefty Grove
Relief pitcher: Ellis Kinder
Manager: Joe McCarthy
Best all-around player: Babe Ruth

# 82 Mo Vaughn

Never underestimate Mo Vaughn's place in Red Sox history. He took his status as an African American player for the Sox very seriously. He understood all too well the team's sordid history of bad race relations dating back to the time Jackie Robinson tried out and wasn't signed by the Red Sox. Vaughn also knew when he arrived in 1991 that Ellis Burks was the only African American player on the team.

He wore No. 42 in honor of Robinson's legacy. His parents, both educators in Norwalk, Connecticut, had known Robinson's widow. Vaughn was a respectful young man who was a number one draft pick out of Seton Hall University. He got his big break on June 27, 1991, when the Red Sox were fading fast in the American League East and needed someone to revive them.

Vaughn was an outspoken, thoughtful man who reenergized the Red Sox during his tenure. He smacked 230 homers in eight seasons in Boston and won the 1995 American League MVP award over Cleveland's Albert Belle in a close vote. Vaughn was thoughtful and intelligent. He fought for all of the right things; winning was very important to him, but he also became a team leader who had a knack for bringing teammates together. Managers Kevin Kennedy and Jimy Williams used him to resolve little skirmishes in the clubhouse.

The front office made him their front man. He was perfect for the job—a guy willing to go out into the African American community who was capable of creating a lot of goodwill for an organization whose involvement with inner-city youth had been so lacking. Vaughn's presence gave disadvantaged youth hope again. He was inspirational as well as giving. He had the same affect on young Red Sox fans that Tony Conigliaro had had some 30 years earlier.

Vaughn touched everyone with his relationship with cancer patient Jason Leader, a young boy who had wanted to talk to Vaughn on the phone. Much to the young boy's surprise, his hero called him. So touched was Vaughn by this brave young man's resolve and optimism that he promised him, "I'm going to hit a home run for you."

This was a Babe Ruth story revisited. Vaughn came up twice and made outs. Then, on his third at-bat, he hit a home run to center field. Vaughn said, "I'm happy for him. I hope he gets strength from that. I hope he learns that dreams can come true." Leader later met Vaughn and sat with him in the dugout before a game. Sadly, the boy died during the next season.

Vaughn's performance on the field was off the charts. From 1993 to 1998 he was one of the most feared hitters in the game. During his MVP season he hit .300 with 39 homers, had 126 RBIs, and had lots of big hits. He did one better in '96 with a .326 average, 44 homers, and 143 RBIs. And in '98 he came within two points of winning a batting title, hitting .337 with 40 homers and 115 RBIs but losing out to the Yankees' Bernie Williams. In an out-of-character performance, he had a terrible '95 playoff series versus the Cleveland Indians, going 0-for-14.

Vaughn got into a contract hassle with the Red Sox after the 1998 season and wound up signing a huge deal with the Anaheim

Angels; his contract was for $88 million over six years. Vaughn hit 69 homers and knocked in 225 runs for the Angels during the next two seasons, but he didn't play in 2001 and was traded to the Mets, where his career ended with a knee injury.

Vaughn now builds low-income housing in Manhattan. In a sad note, in December 2007 he was named in the Mitchell Report as having purchased human growth hormone three times during 2001.

# 83 The One That Got Away

Okay, so 15 seasons, 449 homers, 1,529 RBIs, and a .297 career average later, it can be said that the Red Sox didn't make such a good deal back on August 31, 1990, when they traded third-base prospect Jeff Bagwell to Houston for reliever Larry Andersen. There was no question that the Red Sox needed Andersen. But giving up Bagwell seemed to frost some people at the time.

Nobody could have predicted that Bagwell would become one of the top sluggers in the National League. He had not shown any power in the minors, but he sure could hit. At the time of the deal Bagwell was hitting .333 for Double A New Britain with four homers and 61 RBIs. Nobody hit a lot of homers at Beehive Field in those days because of the weather and the cavernous dimensions of the ballyard.

Asked about the decision to deal Bagwell, Sox CEO John Harrington said, "Two people spoke very passionately that we not give up Bagwell—Joe Morgan and Ed Kenney. Eddie really thought Bagwell was a very good young hitter and he made his case in his usual quiet way. But the consensus of the rest of our people was that we should make the deal because we needed a closer to get us into the postseason."

Lou Gorman's reasoning was that the Red Sox had depth at third base, and he was right about that. They had Tim Naehring, Scott Cooper, and future Hall of Famer Wade Boggs. Butch Hobson, then a manager in the Sox system, planned to move Bagwell to second base in Triple A. At the time of the trade Andersen was lights-out for the Astros, with a 5–2 record, six saves, and a 1.95 ERA; he was considered the best set-up man in baseball. He continued that level of play with the Red Sox, appearing in 15 games after September 1 with a 1.23 ERA and 25 strikeouts over 22 innings. In the playoffs he lost against the Oakland A's. He then left the Red Sox as a free agent and signed with the San Diego Padres in 1991.

Morgan, asked whether the Red Sox gave up too much to get Andersen, said at the time, "We'll find out in the long run. We've got Boggs, Naehring, and Cooper, so we're well stocked. Bagwell is a very aggressive hitter who hits the ball where it's pitched. But he has some work to do at third base."

So the Astros moved him to first, and the rest is history. He won a Gold Glove for the Astros and was named the 1994 National League MVP.

# 84 How Do You Spell Relief?

Red Sox fans tend to get really excited when Jonathan Papelbon comes into a game and strikes out the side for a save in the ninth. But can you imagine sustaining a great relief effort like that over multiple innings, as Ernie Shore, Pedro Martinez, and Dick Radatz did in some incredible individual relief outings?

Shore was normally a starting pitcher. But on June 23, 1917, he entered a game that Babe Ruth had been thrown out of in the first inning and pitched a nine-inning perfect game no-hitter. Ruth had pulled something very similar to the "Possessed Rebel" fit thrown by Roger Clemens in Game 4 of the 1990 playoffs in Oakland. Umpire Brick Owens threatened to throw Ruth out of the game if he didn't shut his yap. But Ruth kept yapping. According to Bill Shannon of *The Boston Post*, Ruth said, "If you run me out of the ballpark, I'll take a punch at you on my way!"

Shore picked off the only base runner of the afternoon, Washington's Ray Morgan, who had been put on base by a walk from Ruth. He retired 26 straight batters after the pickoff, while Ruth was suspended for nine games by Commissioner Ban Johnson and fined a hundred bucks.

Martinez's relief performance in the deciding Game 5 of the 1999 American League Divisional Series against Cleveland was classic. The Sox had come back from an 0–2 deficit to win three straight. They outscored the Indians 44–18 over the final three games, but Martinez saved the day when he entered the Jacobs Field game in Cleveland with the game tied 8–8 and pitched six no-hit innings, striking out eight in the 12–8 win.

Martinez had started Game 1 but had suffered a strained muscle in his back in the process. But after playing catch before the game, he thought he could be available to manager Jimy Williams in relief. Turns out Williams needed him a lot sooner than he thought he would, after the Indians really roughed up Bret Saberhagen and Derek Lowe.

I remember asking Omar Vizquel, who struck out to end the game, about that night. He said, "Honestly, in all of the years I've played major league baseball, I cannot remember when I saw a pitcher do what he [Martinez] did that night. To think he'd been hurt, you'd think he'd be rusty or just not in the groove or something.

You couldn't touch him. I mean, making contact, fouling a ball off, was about all you could hope for."

Travis Fryman was the only batter who got a ball out of the infield, a fly ball out to center field. The Sox also received a seven-RBI performance from Troy O'Leary to help reverse the deficit.

Radatz threw eight and two-thirds scoreless innings in relief of Wilbur Wood on June 11, 1963, coming to the mound with one out and Don Wert on second base. Radatz was so mad at himself after allowing a single to pinch-hitter Bill Bruton in the seventh that his adrenaline took over; from that point on he was like a man possessed.

"I came into the game with a 3–2 lead, and I didn't do my job," said Radatz in 2001. "I have no idea how many pitches I threw. I just wanted to keep pitching. I felt strong and I felt I owed it to the team after I pitched so badly in that situation."

Radatz allowed three hits, walked one, and struck out 11 of the 30 batters he faced, including six of the last eight. He was helped out by Frank Malzone's three-run homer in the fifteenth and a solo shot clubbed by Dick Stuart for a 7–3 win in 15 innings.

# 85 Lights, Camera...NESN

The New England Sports Network, or NESN, has become one of the most profitable regional sports networks around—quite a success story. The Red Sox own 80 percent of the network, the Boston Bruins the other 20 percent. They provide coverage for all Red Sox games that are not exclusively broadcast on national television. The announcers, Don Orsillo and Jerry Remy, have become fixtures in millions of homes across the country. No longer do Red

Sox fans living in Albuquerque or Phoenix or Des Moines have to worry about missing a Red Sox game, even if they are 3,000 miles from Fenway.

This past season the network started quite a bit of original programming. It debuted the popular *Sox Appeal,* a dating show for Red Sox fans set on the rooftop seating area in right field. The premise of the show is to have a single man or woman spend part of a Red Sox game with two or sometimes three potential dates after a meet and greet; the "dates" are captured on film for the show. The person then has to choose which of the "dates" they'd like to see again.

*Red Sox Rewind* is devoted to reviewing the major happenings of the week. There're the pre- and postgame shows hosted by Tom Caron with expert color analysts like Dennis Eckersley, Jim Rice, and Ken Macha breaking down the game. The *Boston Globe Pregame Report* includes *Globe* baseball writers and columnists doing segments and breaking down the news of the day on the Red Sox and the rest of baseball and includes reports from color analyst Jerry Remy. There are pre- and postgame segments with manager Terry Francona and front-office segments with general manager Theo Epstein and president/CEO Larry Lucchino called the *Executive Mailbag.* Tina Cervasio, NESN's on-the-field reporter, checks in before, during, and after the game. During the off-season special old games are rerun on the *Classic Red Sox* program. The weekly *Red Sox Hot Stove* show features a popular "Nine Innings" segment on which a *Globe* sportswriter goes through the top nine topics of the week.

NESN also does a lot of live feeds. They were on the air for two hours to provide live coverage of both the 2004 and 2007 "rolling rallies" through the streets of Boston, complete with fan and player interviews. NESN is live every day from spring training and from baseball's Winter Meetings, and they also go live with press conferences.

*Globe* columnist Bob Ryan's *Globe 10.0* show, broadcast three times a week, is a rapid-fire program featuring *Globe* sportswriters and a local version of ESPN's *Pardon the Interruption* format. The station also does a twice-daily *SportsDesk* show with anchor Hazel Mae, who goes over the local and national sports news.

In the interest of full disclosure, I should mention that I appear on the pregame show for Red Sox telecasts, as well as on other NESN programming, so my opinion may be biased. But I do believe the quality of the Red Sox programming on NESN is top-notch.

# 86 The Idiots

The 2004 Red Sox were a bunch of idiots. Self-professed Idiots, actually, with a capital *I*. The head Idiot was Johnny Damon. The '04 squad was Damon's team, no doubt about it. He set the tone in the clubhouse and on the field for the loosey-goosey style the Red Sox played, and he got his supporting cast—Kevin Millar, Orlando Cabrera, David Ortiz, Manny Ramirez, etc.—to be Idiots as well.

"We are not cowboys anymore," Damon declared during the '04 playoffs, referring to the '03 team's "Cowboy Up" theme, which Millar and Mike Timlin had spun. "We are just the Idiots this year. We feel like we can win every game. We feel like we have fun, and I think that's why this team is liked by so many people out there."

Sox manager Terry Francona thought the Idiots label was a little harsh, but he did say, "As a group, they are borderline nuts, but when they get on the field, I think they try to play the game right."

Ramirez fit this theme perfectly. He even said, "You only live one time. It's easy when you're happy and everything is going good. The days go fast. When you're mad, they go forever." Whatever that meant, it was systematic of what Damon was talking about. Or at least I *think* so, anyway.

Damon and Millar came up with all sorts of schemes and practical jokes during the course of the year. They even got the usually sedate Jason Varitek to go along with most of the pranks. Curt Schilling, Pedro Martinez, Derek Lowe, Bronson Arroyo—they all felt the Idiot label fit the team perfectly.

This was basically a happy-go-lucky team that played hard and never quit. They pulled off the greatest comeback in playoff history, down 3–0 to the Yankees, losing Game 4, and on the verge of elimination before Bill Mueller delivered Dave Roberts with the tying run that fateful night.

"The chemistry on that team was unbelievable," said Cabrera, who joined the Idiots on July 31 in a three-team swap that sent Nomar Garciaparra packing. "We were the Idiots. We were carefree. We just played. We didn't think. We just performed and nothing was too big for us."

Damon, with his long, wavy hair and—during his Idiot years with the Red Sox—his full, bushy beard, never held back when talking to the media. Nor did he hold back when speaking to his teammates when they needed a kick in the pants. "People always need to hear the truth," Damon told *The Boston Globe*. "I'm never going to run away from it. I learned that from Gary Gaetti and Greg Gagne when I first came into the league. Always take the blame when it belongs to you because a lot of people can't."

But despite his carefree spirit, Damon was a player who really cared. Losses really got to him. Wins made him extremely happy. He was happy he was able to act more like an Idiot than anything else in '04.

# 87 John Henry

It was June 13, 2001, in the visitors dugout at Fenway Park. John Henry, then the owner of the Florida Marlins, was in town for an interleague series against the Red Sox. Henry stood looking out at Fenway and remarked to this correspondent, "What a beautiful ballpark. You can just sense the tradition in here." By then Henry knew the Red Sox franchise was for sale—and for all I know he may already have been in discussions with the Yawkey Estate regarding the purchase of the team.

Still, he asked, "Who do you think will buy this team?" I opined to him that I thought perhaps the local ownership group of Joe O'Donnell and Steve Karp would move in, or perhaps Frank McCourt, who owned gorgeous waterfront property in Boston, might emerge to do so. Inside, Henry must have found this amusing.

Henry and his group, which included Tom Werner and *The New York Times*, bid $700 million for the Red Sox and won the auction for the team on February 27, 2002, ending a process that took about a year and a half to complete. The deal had the blessing of Commissioner Bud Selig, and the sale was quickly pushed through—so quickly, in fact, that some media suspected that Selig had promised Henry the team.

Henry had been frustrated by his ownership experience in Florida, where he wasn't able to build a new stadium to make the situation work. He sold the Marlins for about $160 million and applied those funds toward the purchase of the Red Sox. Some of the Sox's limited partners under the Yawkey Estate reinvested with the new ownership. The deal was complicated even further because Major League Baseball had to buy the Montreal Expos from Jeffrey Loria before he could in turn buy the Marlins from Henry. The sale ended 72 years of ownership under the Yawkey name, first by Thomas A. Yawkey, then by his wife, Jean R. Yawkey, and finally by the Yawkey Estate, which was run by John Harrington.

Henry, who made his fortune as a hedge-fund manager, provided tremendous vision for the franchise. With Larry Lucchino on board as the team president and CEO, they even explored the feasibility of a new ballpark. But they soon realized that city politics and the lack of available land would make it almost impossible. They also came to realize that they could use the charm and tradition of Fenway to their advantage.

Gazing out at the ballpark beside Henry that June day in '01 seems like an omen to me now looking back. The Henry group invested millions of dollars in upgrades to Fenway, adding new, fancy seating, including expensive field boxes and the trendy Monster Seats, while also expanding the concourses to set up more fan-friendly seating areas.

Henry, a former limited partner with the New York Yankees, also got quite into the Yankees–Red Sox rivalry, and while unable to match the Yankees payroll (the Red Sox have had the second highest), they certainly went out and became very competitive in the free-agent market, unafraid to spend big money for talent that could compete with their American League East rival.

Henry hired Theo Epstein as general manager and, except for one rough patch after the 2005 season when Epstein declined a three-year, $4.5 million deal and left the team for a few months, the Henry ownership has been very successful, producing two championships in the first five years of their stewardship.

"We have incredibly bright, hardworking, and dedicated people in our organization who work for a common goal of trying to win a championship," Henry said. "Our goal has been to produce a team that can be competitive toward that goal every season. We have devoted resources to scouting and development of our players and we have also been able to explore the free-agent market. We understand the tremendously supportive fan base we have here in Red Sox Nation and we want to give them the best product we can year in and year out."

Henry loves *The Bill James Historical Baseball Abstract*, and he even hired James to be a special adviser for the team. The Henry ownership group has used a combination of the analysis of James's numbers and top scouting to become one of the game's model franchises. The Sox employ more scouts than any team in baseball, and their outside-the-box thinking, as indicated by their $51.1 million posting fee on Japanese pitching star Daisuke Matsuzaka, is an indication of their willingness to search the world for talent.

# 88 He's No Knucklehead

Tim Wakefield will have been in a Red Sox uniform for 14 seasons entering 2008. That's more than Roger Clemens or Cy Young had. Wakefield, a knuckleballer, was rescued off the Pittsburgh Pirates' scrap heap by Dan Duquette early in the 1995 season after being released by the Pirates on April 20. The Red Sox needed pitching because Clemens was injured, so Duquette decided to take a chance on Wakefield.

What a chance it was!

Wakefield rattled off a 14–1 record from May 27—when he made his debut in Anaheim, California—through August 13. He won his Sox debut, 12–1, over the Angels with seven strong innings. He was the savior of the Sox pitching staff, enabling Boston to mount a lead in the American League East. His successful run was similar to a 1992 run he made with the Pittsburgh Pirates, when he went 8–1 with a 2.15 ERA down the stretch

*Knuckleballer Tim Wakefield will have spent 14 seasons in a Red Sox uniform entering 2008. Though his career has suffered some peaks and valleys, Wakefield has been a huge asset to the Red Sox's pitching staff.*

toward a playoff run by the Pirates. Even Barry Bonds commented, "He was our savior." Over that amazing stretch in 1995 he pitched six complete games, including a 10-inning six-hitter in a 2–1 win over Seattle on June 4 in a game in which he threw 135 pitches.

Sox fans have certainly been witness to the unpredictable nature of the knuckleball during Wakefield's career. His performance has suffered through many peaks and valleys. He ended the last nine games of the '95 season 2–7, finishing 16–8 with a 2.95 ERA overall. He also allowed Yankees third baseman Aaron Boone's walk-off homer in Game 7 of the 2003 ALCS, the game in which Grady Little left Pedro Martinez in the game in the eighth inning to squander a three-run lead.

Still, most would agree that Duquette made the right call when he signed Wakefield. He has filled a multitude of roles over the years, bouncing around from starter to bullpen throughout the Jimy Williams years. He saved 15 games for Williams's pitching staff until Derek Lowe replaced him in that assignment, allowing Wakefield to return to his normal role as a starter for good in July 2002. He won 17 games in 1998, 16 in 2005, and 17 in 2007, when his first 26 starts were decisions.

Doug Mirabelli became Wakefield's personal catcher and has caught 169 games for him through the 2007 season (putting him ahead of Jason Varitek, with 146).

Wakefield has always excelled in domed stadiums, but oddly no dome team has ever made a pitch to acquire him. Wakefield is 22–8 at Tropicana Field in St. Petersburg, at the Minneapolis Metrodome, and at Skydome/Rogers Centre in 55 games (as a starter and a reliever).

Wakefield has a unique contract with the Red Sox. In April 2005 he agreed to a rollover one-year contract that stipulates that the team can re-up the agreement for $4 million for as long as they like. It's a good deal for the Red Sox, who would likely have to pay a 17-game winner at least twice that salary on the open market.

# 89 Batting Champs

There's no doubt that hitting has been the strong suit of the Boston Red Sox since 1900. Having a hitter-friendly ballpark since 1912 probably has a lot to do with it. But the Red Sox have consistently won batting titles since Jimmie Foxx earned the team its first of the 20th century in 1938. Interestingly, most of these hitting stars have done their work from the left side of the plate.

It's somewhat surprising that Bill Mueller won a batting title in 2003, since he didn't hit .300 at any other point during his career except for his 200 at-bats as a rookie with the San Francisco Giants. He seemed to thrive on the fact that 303 of his plate appearances came in the number seven and number eight slots, where there wasn't much pressure on him, though he did hit .345 hitting in the second spot in the order in 188 of his plate appearances. He beat out Derek Jeter (.324) and teammate Manny Ramirez (.325) to become the first switch-hitter in Sox history to win a title—and the first in the majors since Bernie Williams in 1998.

"Personal things don't motivate me as much as getting into the playoffs and the World Series," said the much-underappreciated Mueller. He continued his red-hot hitting in the '04 playoffs, driving in Dave Roberts after "the Steal" in Game 4 of the 2004 American League Championship Series versus the Yankees and hitting .429 in the World Series.

Manny Ramirez's .349 average easily outdistanced Kansas City's Mike Sweeney (.340) for the 2002 batting title, which he won with only 120 at-bats because he had missed playing time with a fractured finger incurred on May 11 in Seattle while diving into the plate. Ramirez left the final game of the season, an 11–8 win over the Devil Rays at Fenway, before the game even ended. He was mad at the media because they had chastised him for not running out a ground ball on September 9 at Tampa.

Nomar Garciaparra had an amazing stretch in 1999 and 2000, taking the title in both years. He hit .357 in 1999 to beat out Derek Jeter by eight points during a year in which his offensive performance was overshadowed by Pedro Martinez's tremendous season on the mound. In 2000 he hit .372 to beat runner-up Darin Erstad of the Angels, who hit .355, and Manny Ramirez of the Indians, with .351. There was certainly talk that Garciaparra, a free swinger, might possibly hit .400. He was hitting .403 on July 20 and .398 as late as July 28 before he began to fade.

Wade Boggs's five batting titles (in 1983, 1985, 1986, 1987, and 1988) certainly weren't cheapies. His lowest average in those five seasons was .357 in 1986, while his highest was .368 in 1985. Always incredibly consistent, Boggs also finished second in 1991 and third in 1984 and 1989.

Carney Lansford, who took his title in 1981, was the first right-handed hitter to do so since Alex Johnson in '71. He did it with a .336 average, 10 points over Seattle outfielder Tom Paciorek. Lansford hit .393 in his final 107 at-bats. "Winning this means a helluva lot," he told Peter Gammons of *The Boston Globe*. "When I think of winning a batting title, I think of Rod Carew or Cecil Cooper or Al Oliver. I'd never won any title. Not in the minors or anywhere." Lansford's average was the highest by a right-handed hitter since Harvey Kuenn hit .353 in 1959.

Fred Lynn hit .333 when he bested the injured George Brett by four points for the title in 1979, four years after his 1975 MVP season. As outstanding as his '75 season was, some believe Lynn—who also led the league in slugging (.637) and on-base percentage (.423)—might have been at his finest in 1979. His last hit of the season was his 39th homer.

Carl Yastrzemski won his three batting titles in 1963, 1967, and 1968. The amazing thing about the '67 title is that he had to come from quite far behind to beat Frank Robinson. The Orioles slugger was beating out Yaz with a .331 average (versus Yaz's .308) at the end of August. That's how incredible Yaz's September was; he went on a tear to bring his average up to .326 as part of his Triple Crown season. In 1968 Yaz won with the lowest batting average of any batting title winner in major league history, .301, during the "Year of the Pitcher." Yaz was the only hitter to have an average above .300 in the American League that season. His 1963 batting title came in what many consider to be his breakthrough year as a pro, during which he hit .321.

One of the quieter men in Sox history, Pete Runnels was an infielder who spent five seasons with Boston, two of them as the batting champion—in 1960, when he hit .320, and 1962, at .326. He missed a third title in 1958, finishing six points behind Ted Williams (.328 to .322). Runnels was a singles hitter but still had some memorable feats at the plate, including his performance in one August 30, 1960, doubleheader in which he went 6-for-7 in the first game, with a game-winning RBI double in the fifteenth inning, and 3-for-4 in the nightcap. A career .291 hitter, Runnels was a three-time All-Star who also served as an interim manager for the final 16 games of the 1966 season.

Billy Goodman, who won his title in 1950, was a left-handed batter who spent 10 years with the Red Sox and hit .300 for his career. He had his best year in 1950, batting .354 to lead the American League. He also finished second to Yankees shortstop Phil Rizzuto in the MVP voting that year.

Ted Williams, "the Splendid Splinter," won batting titles in 1941, 1942, 1947, 1948, 1957, and 1958. The greatest of those four seasons was obviously 1941, when he hit .406; to this day he is still the last man in Major League Baseball to ever hit .400. In 1958, at age 40, Williams hit a whopping .388, an accomplishment so amazing that some observers even allowed themselves to fantasize that Williams might be able to hit .400 again.

In 1938—one of the greatest Red Sox seasons ever—Jimmie Foxx hit .349, winning the Red Sox's first batting title of the 20th century. Foxx was a devastating hitter as well as an outstanding overall player, also winning the league's MVP award for the season.

The Sox acquired Dale Alexander from Detroit in 1932, the same year he won his batting title. He played 23 games for the Tigers before spending the rest of the season with Boston. He hit .372 for the '32 Red Sox—the worst team in franchise history— and his .367 overall batting average led the American League.

# 90 Dan Duquette

Despite the bad feelings he inspired in so many people, "the Duke" made more than a few significant contributions to the Red Sox. He's the man who swung a deal for Pedro Martinez (who was traded in exchange for Carl Pavano and Tony Armas Jr.) in November 1997, ushering in a very exciting era in Boston. He also made two great deals that helped the Red Sox win two championships after his tenure: he signed Manny Ramirez to an eight-year, $160 million contract prior to the 2002 season, and he brought Derek Lowe and captain Jason Varitek to Boston in 1997 in exchange for closer Heathcliff Slocomb. Duquette also signed Johnny Damon, who was instrumental in the '04 championship, to a free-agent contract. Of course Duquette will also forever be known as the man who let Roger Clemens and Mo Vaughn leave Boston and who brought the divisive Carl Everett to town.

Duquette also developed a reputation for being cold. He let many longtime staffers go. He even clashed with his own hand-picked manager, Kevin Kennedy, who won the division in 1995.

Their relationship was so bad that they had to go to an independent counselor to try to work out their differences. It didn't work, and Kennedy was let go after the '96 season.

There were a lot of people who didn't want to be around the ballpark during the eight years that Duquette was in charge. For a kid who had grown up in Dalton, Massachusetts, as a Red Sox fan, and who later earned an excellent reputation with his work for the small-market Montreal Expos, Duquette's behavior was considered quite strange by many.

John Henry and Larry Lucchino informed Duquette that his tenure was over on February 28, 2002, shortly after they took over the team. Duquette announced his departure at his resort hotel on Sanibel Island, Florida, weeping during his farewell speech.

Duquette showed up during the 2004 Series to do some TV work. He said at the time, "I'm very happy for this. Above everything, I'm a Red Sox fan. I've been a fan since I was a kid growing up in this area, so I'm able to step back from it and enjoy it as a fan."

# 91 The Citgo Sign

Although it's actually located at 660 Beacon Street in Kenmore Square, the Citgo sign is one of the landmarks most closely associated with Fenway Park and the Red Sox. In fact, when fans drive to Fenway, they can tell if they're in the general area of the ballpark based on whether or not they can see it. The sign, about 60 feet tall and 60 feet wide, contains about 5,900 neon lights, which illuminate part of the Charles River at night.

"CITGO holds an especially important place in Boston," the Citgo website reads. "The illuminated sign in Kenmore Square has

*The Citgo sign in Kenmore Square is a landmark that lets Red Sox fans know they are nearing Fenway Park. The sign, which measures 60 feet tall and 60 feet wide and is comprised of over 5,900 neon lights, was refurbished by Citgo in recent years because of its historic significance to the Red Sox Nation.* Photo courtesy of AP/Wide World Photos.

become a landmark on the Boston skyline. It graces left field at Fenway Park and has seen thousands of athletes to the finish line at the Boston Marathon. It also serves as an excellent orientation point when people are lost in the city."

Once in the ballpark fans can see the Citgo sign beyond the Green Monster at about left-center, starting about halfway up the old-fashioned wooden scoreboard. You can't miss it. Its red, white, and blue design is eye-catching to say the least, especially when it is lit up at night. Every time a ball is hit to left field, you see the Citgo sign.

The sign actually advertised the Cities Services company when it was erected in 1940, but when the company changed its name in 1965, the sign changed as well. It was turned off in 1979 when then-governor Edward J. King was on an energy conservation kick, and it wasn't turned back on again until four years later. At one point Citgo wanted to dismantle the sign, but there were so many protests that they decided to refurbish it instead, pouring about a million dollars into the landmark.

Only one time since has anyone suggested that the Citgo sign be taken down for any reason. Citgo is a subsidiary of Venezuela's state-owned oil company, Petroleos de Venezuela S.A. (PDVSA). In 2006, after Venezuelan president Hugo Chavez called President George W. Bush the devil, one Boston city councilor thought the sign should be taken down to protest Chavez's words. The suggestion did not receive much support.

Another huge landmark at Fenway is the "Coke Bottles" advertisement in left field, which is also quite large and can't be missed. The Prudential building can also be seen beyond right field.

# 92 Hey Lefty

The myth—or perhaps it still isn't a myth in the minds of some—is that lefties can't pitch well at Fenway Park. In fact, the Yankees went out of their way not to start Hall of Famer Whitey Ford at Fenway, feeling that with Boston's excellent right-handed hitters and the Wall to contend with, it just wasn't fair. Ford was 4–5 with a 6.44 ERA at Fenway in 11 games and nine starts, allowing seven home runs in 50⅓ innings from 1957 to 1963.

But the Red Sox had many left-handed pitchers who did just fine at Fenway. Babe Ruth was one. Lefty Grove, Mel Parnell, Bill Lee, and Bruce Hurst also didn't seem to have difficulty there.

Lefty Grove was 41 years old in 1941, heading to the end of a glorious career. "He was still quite a show every time he pitched," Dom DiMaggio remembered. "For as many things that happened in that incredible year of 1941, Lefty getting his 300th win (on July 25) was right up there with all of it. He was so respected. Such a classy individual. We were all proud to have played with him."

Grove's best seasons were with Philadelphia, where he won two championships and 31 games in 1931. Connie Mack, trying to dump some of his high-priced players, sold Grove off to the Red Sox in 1933, and despite a sore arm he won 105 games with Boston. He won 20 games only once, yet his record was good enough to make him Boston's second winningest lefty (behind Mel Parnell). He had a 55–17 record at Fenway—definitely not shabby. Joe Cronin once commented about Grove: "He was great at getting the first man out in ninth-inning situations when the Sox were protecting a one-run lead." He also developed a great curveball while he was with Boston.

Grove just barely won his 300th game at Fenway before calling it quits. Dom DiMaggio remembers, "He still had one of the best curveballs in the game. You'd just see a lot of frustrated faces going back to the dugout after facing Lefty. Even though he was up there in age by that point, he was an event. He was a guy that everyone loved and respected because of what he had done and the respect he had for the game of baseball."

Without question Mel Parnell's great record shatters the myth that lefties can't win at Fenway. Parnell, raised in New Orleans (where he still lives), flourished at Fenway with a 71–30 record there (he was 123–75 overall during his 10 seasons in the game). He won

25 in 1949. "For me the strategy was simple," Parnell said. "You had to pitch inside to right-handed hitters so they couldn't extend their arms and take you deep. I changed the way I pitched from the minors to the majors when I saw the ballpark. In the minors I threw mostly fastballs, but when I started pitching at Fenway, I threw mostly curves and sliders because I wanted the movement on the ball to ride in on a right-handed hitter and stay low. I never nibbled outside because if I missed, it would be over the plate."

Bill Lee had three consecutive 17-win seasons from 1973 to 1975. His finesse style, keeping hitters off balance and allowing hitters to hit to the larger parts of Fenway, made Lee extremely effective. "You just learn to pitch and you learn how to set up hitters," Lee explained. "Pitching at Fenway wasn't something I was ever in awe of. I could never understand why a lefty couldn't pitch there."

Bruce Hurst also had three excellent seasons, from 1986 to 1988, with 13–8, 15–13, and 18–6 records, before leaving to sign with San Diego as a free agent in 1989. After his career was over, Hurst admitted, "I wished I'd never left Boston." Hurst, too, had a tremendous knack for busting right-handed hitters inside so they couldn't extend their arms. He also had enough of a fastball that he could overpower hitters. When he was on, he was masterful, sporting a superb curveball that simply buckled hitters.

# 93 Colorful Characters

There have always been guys with the Sox who were just a little bit different—a little on the dark side, or a little zany.

Jimmy Piersall immediately comes to mind. The movie *Fear Strikes Out* tells his story, and though there were a few things in it that were exaggerated or altered for Hollywood, the essence of it is true. Piersall, by all accounts a tremendous center fielder, had a mental health issue that resulted in his hospitalization.

Originally a shortstop, the Sox moved Piersall to center field when GM Joe Cronin acquired Johnny Lipon from the Tigers. While Ted Williams commented that Piersall was the best center fielder he'd ever seen—and Williams had just spent 10 years watching Dom DiMaggio at that position—the move wasn't easy for Piersall, who was very nervous about playing a new position. He started acting strangely in a June 12, 1952, game against the St. Louis Browns. He began by mimicking Satchel Paige, then started snorting like a pig while at first base after he told Paige that he was going to get a bunt off him. There were other incidents of that kind. Piersall also engaged in a fistfight with Yankees infielder Billy Martin, with Martin bloodying Piersall, after the two had exchanged insults.

"I'm crazy and I got the papers to prove it," Piersall said jokingly in numerous interviews over the years. In a book about his life he wrote, "The crack-up was probably the best thing that ever happened to me. Who ever heard of Jimmy Piersall before that happened?"

Bill "Spaceman" Lee, a successful lefty at Fenway, was also both controversial and humorous. He often battled with manager Don Zimmer, calling him "the Gerbil." He repeatedly clashed with the Yankees as well, particularly Graig Nettles. Lee accused Nettles of separating Lee's shoulder in a bench-clearing brawl on May 20, 1976, after a Carlton Fisk–Lou Piniella home-plate collision.

The modern-day Satchel Paige, Dennis "Oil Can" Boyd underwent a psychological evaluation after he erupted when he was left off the All-Star team in 1986. Boyd, who was a suspected drug user during his years with the Red Sox, was also bypassed for a Game 7 start in the 1986 World Series; he cried over the news that he would be replaced by Bruce Hurst. Once, after a game with the Cleveland

Indians at the old Municipal Stadium was called because of severe fog, Boyd said, "That's what they get for building a ballpark on the ocean." (Municipal Stadium was in fact built along Lake Eerie, as Cleveland is of course nowhere near the ocean.)

Carl Everett was another player with bizarre behavioral tendencies; he denounced gays and also questioned the existence of dinosaurs. In 2000 he had a classic meltdown because umpire Ron Kulpa told him he was using an illegal batting stance. Everett then head-butted the umpire, receiving a 10-game suspension in response.

# 94 Hot Stove Dinner

As big as the regular season and the postseason are in Red Sox Nation, the Hot Stove season is also a huge sport in and of itself. Red Sox fans often spend a great deal of time glued to their computers, televisions, newspapers, and radios each winter, hoping to hear the latest trade rumor or anything that relates to the next season.

Smack in the middle of the winter, a few weeks before pitchers and catchers report to Fort Myers, die-hard Red Sox fans attend the Boston Baseball Writers Dinner, which is normally held on the third Thursday in January. The dinner's tremendous head table is filled with award winners from the previous season chosen by the Boston baseball writers. If a player has received a national award, he is usually honored at the dinner, which is held each year at an exclusive ballroom in a Boston hotel.

Many of the greatest Red Sox players in history—including Ted Williams, Bobby Doerr, Carl Yastrzemski, Jim Rice, Wade Boggs, and Roger Clemens, among others—as well as players and front-office executives from all over baseball including Commissioner Bud Selig, have attended the dinner over the years. There are of course many funny and moving speeches during the course of the evening. There's also usually a time set aside for an autograph session during which grown men and their sons or daughters can step up to the head table to have their favorite player—or simply the entire dais—sign their program or baseball.

Boston's finest baseball writers—including Bill Ballou of the *Worcester Telegram & Gazette*; Sean McAdam and Steve Krasner of *The Providence Journal*; Michael Silverman, Jeff Horrigan, Tony Massarotti, Steve Buckley, and Rob Bradford of the *Boston Herald*; and Gordon Edes, Amalie Benjamin, Dan Shaughnessy, and Bob Ryan of *The Boston Globe*, among others—attend the dinner every year. The late Larry Whiteside is a past chairman of the organization, while Hall of Fame baseball writer Peter Gammons attended many dinners over the years when he was with *The Boston Globe* and later for *Sports Illustrated* and ESPN.

Every season the writers honor a longtime baseball personage for meritorious service to the sport with the Judge Emil Fuchs Award. (Fuchs was one of the owners of the now-defunct Boston Braves.) There's also the Dave O'Hara Award, which is handed out every season to a longtime Boston baseball writer. The annual Tony Conigliaro Award, given to the major league player who has shown the most courage and determination in overcoming some obstacle in his life, is issued at the dinner as well. In 2007 it went to cancer survivor Jon Lester, while another cancer survivor, Mike Lowell, was honored the year before that.

This special evening is usually the last major off-season event before the Red Sox pack up their trucks and move everything south to Fort Myers.

# 95 The Red Sox Hall of Fame

Someday, when the Red Sox can find some room somewhere in the tiny footprint of Fenway Park, there'll actually be a home for the Red Sox Hall of Fame. But for now the Sports Museum of New England plays home to the Hall as it were. The Hall was begun in 1995; inductees are selected by a 15-man committee made up of broadcasters, executives, past and present media, representatives of the Sports Museum, and the BoSox Club (the team's official fan club).

The inductees are honored at an annual dinner in Boston that attracts big crowds of Sox fans looking to see and applaud stars of yesteryear. All players who have been enshrined in Cooperstown with Red Sox ties are automatically inducted into the Red Sox Hall. Players are required to have played at least three years with the Red Sox and must be out of uniform for at least three years before they can be inducted. Nonuniformed personnel are inducted by the Boston Red Sox Hall of Fame selection committee. A "Memorable Moment" is also selected every year.

Hall of Famers automatically inducted into the Red Sox Hall include Eddie Collins, Jimmy Collins, Joe Cronin, Bobby Doerr, Rick Ferrell, Jimmie Foxx, Curt Gowdy, Lefty Grove, Harry Hooper, Babe Ruth, Tris Speaker, Ted Williams, Carl Yastrzemski, longtime owner Tom Yawkey, and Cy Young.

The inductees since 1995 have been Dick Bresciani, Rick Burleson, Bill Carrigan, Ken Coleman, Tony Conigliaro, Dom DiMaggio, Dwight Evans, Dave "Boo" Ferriss, Larry Gardner, Billy Goodman, Lou Gorman, John Harrington, Tex Hughson, Bruce Hurst, Jackie Jensen, Ellis Kinder, Duffy Lewis, Jim Lonborg, Fred Lynn, Frank Malzone, Ned Martin, Bill Monbouquette, Ben

Mondor, Joe Morgan, Dick O'Connell, Mel Parnell, Johnny Pesky, Rico Petrocelli, Dick Radatz, Jerry Remy, Jim Rice, Pete Runnels, George Scott, Reggie Smith, Bob Stanley, Vern Stephens, Haywood Sullivan, Luis Tiant, Dick Williams, Smoky Joe Wood, and Jean R. Yawkey.

The current "Memorable Moments" are Roger Clemens's first 20-strikeout game, in 1986; Carlton Fisk's game-winning home run during the 1975 World Series; Dave Henderson's game-changing home run in Game 5 of the 1986 American League Championship Series; Earl Wilson's no-hitter on June 26, 1962; Bernie Carbo's pinch-hit homer in Game 6 of the 1975 World Series; and Dave Roberts's steal of second base in Game 4 of the 2004 American League Championship Series.

# 96 Ted's Memories Frozen in Time

If you're in the St. Petersburg area or taking in a Sox-Rays game at Tropicana Field, why not stop by the Ted Williams Museum and Hitters Hall of Fame. Why isn't this in Boston? Got any space at or around Fenway you'd like to rent out?

The museum features many artifacts devoted to Williams's military service in World War II and the Korean conflict in addition to those from his exploits as the greatest hitter who ever lived. But there's more than Williams. There are also displays and exhibits devoted to Willie Mays and Hank Aaron, Roger Maris, Mickey Mantle, and Japanese home-run champ Sadaharu Oh. The museum's executive director is Dave McCarthy, a former New Hampshire state police detective who always loved all things Ted Williams. He helped move the museum from Hernando, Florida

*This statue of Ted Williams greets all visitors to the Ted Williams Museum and Hitters Hall of Fame in Hernando, Florida.* Photo courtesy of AP/Wide World Photos.

(not far from Williams's Florida home), to its current more spacious facility near Tropicana Field.

There's a touching tribute to Larry Hawkins, the man who saved Williams's life in North Korea. Williams's plane had been hit by enemy fire and when it began to smoke, Williams became disoriented and flew deeper into the enemy zone. Hawkins tracked Williams down and pulled up alongside him, signaling for Williams to follow him back to safety.

Visiting Scottsdale? Drive by the Alcor Life Extension Foundation, where Williams's frozen body is stored in a cryonic facility in the hopes that science will someday be able to revive him and he will walk the Earth again. Williams's body was brought to the lab on July 5, 2002, after his heart stopped. The lab is located on East Acoma Drive at Scottsdale Airpark, but you won't be allowed in. Williams's son, John Henry Williams, who died of leukemia, is also there. It was decided by Williams's children John Henry and Claudia that Ted's body would be frozen in time rather than buried. The decision was fought at the time by Williams's other daughter, Bobby-Jo Williams Ferrell, but John Henry and Claudia won out after a legal battle in which it was ruled that freezing the body was what Williams wanted, as indicated by his will.

# 97 Others I Should Mention

Like I said, space is limited here, but there are few other players fans need to have some knowledge about if they want to call themselves true Red Sox aficionados.

Walter Johnson was once asked if he could throw harder than Smoky Joe Wood. Johnson's response? "Listen, mister, no man alive can throw any harder than Smoky Joe Wood." Wood had the greatest season of any Red Sox pitcher in history, going 34–5 with a 1.91 ERA and 10 shutouts in 1912. He notched a 3–1 record in the World Series, including the clinching game in the best-of-eight series, outthrowing Christy Mathewson. His signature moment came on September 6, 1912, versus Johnson. Wood was only 22 years old when he beat Johnson 1–0.

I remember speaking to Wood at a reunion of the greatest Red Sox players at Fenway in 1985, a year before his death at age 95. Wood's memory had faded, but he recalled the game. "That was the only game I remember at Fenway Park, or anywhere else for that matter. The fans were practically sitting along the first-base line and the third-base line."

Jimmy Collins managed the 1903 World Series, and he also led the Sox to first place in '04, when the World Series was suspended for a year. He was an outstanding player as well. He was known for his ability to run down pop-ups along the third-base line. He was also known for his intelligence, which is probably why he became a manager. He helped to thwart a Pittsburgh rally in the fourth inning of the deciding game of the 1903 World Series when he pulled off a fake pickoff play that led to a runner being picked off second base.

Jackie Jensen's career was cut short at the dawn of the age of air travel because he feared flying, but he still made quite an impact. He won the 1958 American League MVP with 35 homers and 122 RBIs. He had five seasons with the Red Sox in which he knocked in 100 or more runs. He was a terrific right fielder with a great arm and was a Gold Glove winner. He was also a star halfback at the University of California and played in the Rose Bowl, becoming the first player to compete in both the Rose Bowl and the World Series. The Boston Baseball Writers Association hands out the Jackie Jensen Award for "spirit and determination" on an annual basis.

Frank Malzone was a three-time Gold Glove winner at third base. He made six All-Star teams in his 10-year career. A native of the Bronx, Malzone started his career with the Sox in 1955 but didn't become a full-time player until 1957. Malzone, currently a player development consultant with the team, also served as a long-time talent and advance scout for the Red Sox.

"The Steamer," Bob Stanley, holds the Red Sox record for games pitched (637), saves (132), and games finished (376). He also holds the American League record for relief innings pitched with 168⅔ in 1982. He's also the guy who threw the wild pitch in Game 6 of the 1986 World Series, scoring Kevin Mitchell from third base and advancing Ray Knight to second base before Mookie Wilson's ground ball went through Bill Buckner's legs. He also allowed what proved to be the game-winning homer in the 1978 playoff game versus the Yankees, an eighth-inning homer by Reggie Jackson that gave the Yanks their fifth run in their eventual 5–4 win.

# 98 The Strangest Thing I Ever Saw

When I was covering the Yankees-Cleveland divisional playoff series in 2007—watching as tiny midges attacked Yankees rookie reliever Joba Chamberlain—it brought me back to May 27, 1986, and a game played at the old Municipal Stadium in Cleveland. The Red Sox won the fog-shortened contest 2–0 before 6,661 fans who must have had considerable difficulty finding their cars in the parking lot after the game.

The fog was so thick that I had to have a police officer help me find my own vehicle. Driving was hazardous because visibility was nil. The fog was so thick that if there was a shallow pop fly hit into the outfield, the infielder would disappear beyond the infield dirt and wouldn't reappear until he came back into view on the infield.

The weird thing is that the evening began with a clear sky. The Sox scored twice in the first inning with run-producing singles by Bill Buckner and Jim Rice. By the fifth inning, however, fog began to roll in off Lake Erie like something out of an Alfred Hitchcock thriller. Umpire Larry Barnett delayed the game twice, once for eight minutes and then again for 95 minutes. During the delays players would appear on the field and then vanish off into the outfield fog.

During the first delay Cleveland first-base coach Bobby Bonds hit fungoes as a test to see whether the outfielders could see the ball. Dwight Evans lost a couple while the umpires stood next to him to see if *they* could locate the ball. The umpires resumed play when the fog seemed to lighten up, but it soon became just as bad once again. In the sixth inning, Indians outfielder Mel Hall hit a long fly ball to center field, and Tony Armas Jr. really had to struggle to see it as he went back to catch it against the wall.

This was worse than direct sunlight in your eyes. The fog never lifted, just moving closer and closer to the pitcher's mound until those of us in the press box could only see from the batter's box to just beyond the mound. Everything else was a sea of white puffiness. The outfielders had to basically anticipate where the ball would be and hope they could react at the last minute when they finally caught a glimpse of it through the fog. That's when the umpires called the second delay. By then, there had been enough innings played to make the game official, and the Red Sox won it, 2–0.

After the game players shook their heads in disbelief about what they had just witnessed. The evening prompted Dennis Boyd to utter his famous line, "That's what they get for building a ballpark on the ocean."

I walked out of the ballpark that night with the late Larry Whiteside. He asked me, "Where's your car?" I said, "Tell me where the parking lot is first." At that point a police car came by; the officer said, "Hop in," and helped us find our vehicles.

# 99 A Comeback Worth Remembering

Boston's comeback from a 2–0 deficit in the best-of-five divisional playoff series versus Cleveland in 1999 was pretty impressive. After losing two straight games, Sox manager Jimy Williams was asked what he was going to do to avoid elimination. Said Williams, "I don't know. Maybe I'll just get ahold of George Herman Ruth. I don't know. What do you want me to do?"

Rather than trying to channel the Babe, Williams instead made the most of John William Valentin, Troy Franklin O'Leary, and Robert Michael Stanley. Stanley in fact hit .500 in the series, going 10-for-20. The Red Sox tied the series up with a record-setting 23–7 win over the Indians to send it back to Cleveland. Valentin drove in seven runs in Game 4, and O' Leary knocked out seven runs in Game 5 with a pair of homers, including a grand slam. Before their Game 3 win to avoid elimination, the Sox had previously lost 18 of their last 19 postseason games. But the Red Sox outscored the Indians 44–18 over the final three games of this Series despite the fact that top slugger Mo Vaughn and closer Tom Gordon were out of action with injuries.

In Game 4 the Sox exploded at Fenway, scoring runs in every inning except the sixth. Rookie Trot Nixon's two-run double in the seventh shattered the record for runs in a postseason game, a mark set during the 1936 World Series when Lou Gehrig and Joe DiMaggio paced the Yankees to an 18–4 win over the New York Giants. Stanley stroked five of Boston's 24 hits, also a record.

Valentin's seven RBIs came as a result of two homers, a double, and a single.

The Sox won the clinching game 12–8 on an incredible relief performance from Pedro Martinez, who pitched six no-hit innings after suffering a strained muscle in his back in Game 1; it had been very questionable if he would be able to pitch again in this series. But oh, he did. Manager Jimy Williams had been thrilled to hear that Martinez would be able to pitch in Game 5, although he thought Martinez would be good for only a couple of innings, tops. But Martinez was on fire—unhittable. With Martinez on the mound, the Sox bounced back from the mammoth homers hit by Jim Thome that ran starter Bret Sabherhagen and then reliever Derek Lowe out of the game. The game was over when O'Leary made the Indians' Paul Shuey pay for walking Nomar Garciaparra to get to him. O'Leary responded with a three-run homer that broke open an 8–8 tie in the seventh. O'Leary had hit a grand slam against Charles Nagy in the third, more than making up for his 1-for-16 performance against the Tribe in the 1998 playoffs.

The Sox had earned the right to face the New York Yankees in the American League Championship Series. But they soon came back down to Earth, losing four out of five games to the men in pinstripes to be eliminated.

# 100 Wally the Green Monster

When Red Sox mascot Wally the Green Monster made his debut on April 13, 1997, purists and traditionalists asked why. But when you get to know the big, green, furry guy and watch his act, he's pretty entertaining. In fact, he's been quite a hit with the children's

*Wally the Green Monster, the Red Sox mascot for over 10 years, is revered in Boston both on and off the field.* Photo courtesy of AP/Wide World Photos.

segment of Red Sox Nation, and, quite frankly, even some of us older kids get a kick out of him.

Wally has also become quite popular away from Fenway. He can be hired for birthday parties and other social events—when he's not busy at the ballpark, that is, which he is during every home game. Wally occasionally does some traveling with the team as well, especially to those games where a heavy dose of Red Sox fans are expected.

Here are Wally's stats:

Height: Pretty big
Weight: Doesn't like to say
Color: Green
Favorite vacation spot: Fort Myers (every March)
Residence: The Green Monster, Fenway Park
Favorite Song: "Dirty Water"

Back on August 3, 2007, some of us wondered what—or who—had gotten into Wally. Turns out it was Sox chairman Tom Werner. Wally's "coat" was intercepted by Werner, who got into the Wally costume to play a prank on president Larry Lucchino. According to the *Boston Globe*, Werner went up to Lucchino on the field before a game and started messing with him, slamming against him and even putting up his dukes to fight. Lucchino kept asking, "What are you doing!" thinking Wally had gone a little haywire. Werner finally fessed up to his prank and told Lucchino (through the Wally outfit), "Larry, it's me, Tom."